MW01622278

HISTORIC WILLIAMSON COUNTY

An Illustrated History

by John J. Leffler

Published for the Williamson County Historical Commission

Historical Publishing Network
A division of Lammert Publications, Inc.
San Antonio, Texas

Trade Days in Taylor, c. 1920s.

COURTESY OF THE TAYLOR PUBLIC LIBRARY.

First Edition

ISBN: 1-893619-09-5

Library of Congress Card Catalog Number: 00-106327

Historic Williamson County: An Illustrated History

author: John J. Leffler

cover artist: Dalhart Windberg

contributing writer for "sharing the heritage": Judy Trice

Historical Publishing Network

president: Ron Lammert

vice president: Barry Black

project manager: Pat Steele

director of operations: Charles A. Newton, III

administration: Angela Lake
Donna Mata
Dee Steidle

graphic production: Colin Hart
John Barr

PRINTED IN SINGAPORE

Contents

❖

Main Street, Florence, 1910.

COURTESY OF THE WILLIAMSON COUNTY HISTORICAL COMMISSION AND DANNELLY BROWN.

PREFACE

For about ten years I taught at Southwestern University and traveled up I-35 from Austin to Georgetown almost every day; but though one of the courses I taught was Texas history, I knew almost nothing about Williamson County. Then, about three years ago, I was asked to write a history of the area for a special sesquicentennial edition of the *Austin American-Statesman*. As part of my research, I spent many days travelling around the county with local historians Ralph Dixon Love and Martha Mitten Allen, and came to see a side of the county and its people—and a side of life—that I had never been able to notice before.

Visiting the past, the historian Carl Becker observed, is like touring a foreign country. Look at the photographs in this book. The people in them lived in a society in many ways very different from our own; it was a world most of us have to study to understand, and which exists now only in memory and imagination. Nevertheless the scenes and faces often seem strangely familiar. Scattered all around us today are reminders of an intimate, community-oriented way of life that has been fading for some time and now seems in danger of being swept away by rapid development, new industries, and the atomized fast pace of modern American life. But as William Faulkner once wrote, "The past isn't dead; it isn't even past." Ideas, attitudes, and actions almost invisible to us now continue to shape the patterns of our lives and our understanding of who we are. The photos tell their own stories, but I hope my overview history of the county will help to bring them into sharper focus.

John J. Leffler

George White and his family, farming north of Liberty Hill.

PHOTO COURTESY OF THE WILLIAMSON COUNTY HISTORICAL COMMISSION AND JEANNE MCNABB.

Acknowledgments

I can't adequately express my thanks to the many people who have contributed in so many ways to this book. It grew out of the 1998 *Austin American-Statesman* sesquicentennial project, and would never have been written without the help I received from the Williamson County Sesquicentennial Committee. Several members of the Committee, particularly Martha Allen, Hugh Davenport, Lester Fisher, Della Green, Rod Johnson, Leslie Hill, Ralph Dixon Love, and Irene Varan generously gave many hours of their time to contribute to the sesquicentennial project in various ways. Hugh Davenport, Lester Fisher, Della Green, and Leslie Hill were very kind to me; each of them spent hours sharing their knowledge of the county's history and culture, and freely gave me the fruits of their own research. Irene Varan helped me find photographs and sources, passed on historical materials, and spent days of her own time to make the Williamson County Historical Commission's extensive scrapbook collection accessible to me. Martha Mitten Allen's contributions of her time, knowledge, and editorial expertise were indispensable. Ralph Dixon Love generously spent many days touring the county with me, sharing his remarkable knowledge of the county's history, culture, and folklore. Walter Brewer of the *Austin American-Statesman* put the whole thing together with patience, intelligence, and skill.

Since then, in preparing this book, I fell into even deeper debt. Irene Varan of the Williamson County Historical Commission kindly helped me in many ways, large and small; she and Martha Allen both read the manuscript, saving me from a number of mistakes and improving my prose. James and Hazel Hood, Rod Johnson, and George Meyer each contributed many hours of their time to make the Historical Commission's photograph collection available to me, and shared their own historical photos and materials; George Meyer also tracked down some of the original donors of the photos to get more information about them.

Many other people have also shared their photographs, knowledge, and historical materials or contributed to the book in other ways. During a remarkable series of photoshoots conducted by the Sesquicentennial Committee and the Institute of Texan Cultures in 1998, scores of Williamson County residents allowed their family photos to be copied; over a hundred of those pictures appear in this volume. Thanks also to Michael Collins (Texas Archeological Research Laboratory), Sondra Carlton (Sun City), Patsy Crossley, Gael Dillard (Georgetown Heritage Society), LaVerne Faubian, Virginia and Emily Foster, Mike Fowler, Shelly Hargrove (Taylor Main Street Program), Irene Michna, J. C. Johnson, Joan Kilpatrick and Galen Greaser (Texas General Land Office), Karen Halford, Dan Martinets, Ethel Mickan, Mark Odintz (Texas State Historical Association), Tom Shelton (Institute of Texan Cultures), Leon Schrank (Williamson County Farm Service Bureau), Frances Shell, and Walter Thoms. Thanks also to the librarians, archivists, and staff at the Georgetown, Round Rock, Taylor, and Austin public libraries; the Austin History Center; the Texas State Library and Archives; the Perry Castenada Library and the Center for American History at the University of Texas-Austin; and at the Round Rock, Cedar Park, and Taylor Chambers of Commerce.

I dedicate this book to my wonderful parents, Jean and Jack Leffler.

Before air conditioning, people often slept on their porches to keep cool in the hot summer months. This picture of a three-room, board-and-batten farmhouse was taken near Andice in 1915.

COURTESY OF THE WILLIAMSON COUNTY HISTORICAL COMMISSION AND CONNIE KANETSKY.

Andrew Janak and his family at the Hermina Janak home southwest of Granger about 1896.

COURTESY OF THE WILLIAMSON COUNTY HISTORICAL COMMISSION AND DOLORES MACHEE VOLEK.

❖

A group of Tonkawa Indians in 1898. Seated at the center is Chief Grant Richards.

COURTESY OF THE TONKAWA TRIBE OF OKLAHOMA.

Before Settlement: Early Inhabitants

PREHISTORICAL PEOPLES

Americans tend to measure their history in decades, or centuries—houses in central Texas are considered "old" if they were built a hundred years ago. But people have been living and dying in the Williamson County area for at least 12,000 years, and evidence of the indigenous peoples who once lived here can be found all around.

The rather mysterious people who first moved into the Williamson County area probably arrived during the late Pleistocene period, when the local habitat was much different than it is today. The weather then was considerably wetter and colder, the trees larger, the vegetation more lush. Mammoths wandered across the landscape along with other mammals, including bison, foxes, coyotes, and skunks. The first Paleoindian inhabitants of the area used a wide variety of local resources to sustain themselves. They made spears with sharp stone points to hunt large animals like the mammoth and the bison, but much of their diet consisted of smaller animals like turtles, fish, foxes, and rodents. They also made a number of different tools, like scrapers and sewing needles, and created jewelry out of materials like animal teeth and turtle shells. The Paleoindians apparently buried their dead with ceremony and care.

Archaeologists working near Leander in the 1980s uncovered the remains of a woman buried about 10,500 years ago; she had died when she was about thirty years old. Her skeleton, discovered at what is now known as the Wilson-Leonard site, is one of the twelve oldest ever found in the Western hemisphere.

Pleistocene mammals like the mammoth became extinct in central Texas about 10,000 years ago, possibly because a sudden climatic change left many parts of North America hotter and drier than before. Over the next few thousand years new technologies evolved as people worked to adapt to new conditions. Archeologists have noted that about 8,500 years ago—near the beginning of what is known as the Archaic period—some people in central Texas abruptly shifted to using stone-lined earth ovens to cook their vegetables. At the Wilson-Leonard site, onion-like bulbs have been found well-preserved in what is left of some of these ovens. Burned rock middens, found throughout Williamson County, are enduring evidence of the ovens and the Archaic people who used them.

Through much of the Archaic period, which lasted about 6,000 years, the climate of central Texas seems to have become hotter and less humid: the area became primarily covered with grasslands, interspersed with clumps of live oak and other trees. The change was so slow that people living in the area probably had few problems adapting to the gradual shifts in their environment. During the Archaic period people also began to use new hunting and gathering strategies and technologies to help them live from the land. Because roots, nuts, seeds and fruits (and maybe insects) became more important to the diet of people who lived during this time, grinding stones (called *manos*) and grinding surfaces (called *metates*) are often found in areas inhabited then. A variety of new projectile points were devised to tip darts and light spears to kill small animals; hunters used spearthrowers (called *atlatls*) to hurl their weapons into their prey.

People living in the Williamson County area at that time also seem to have adapted their diets to the new conditions in another way: they ate more fish. As the habitats of "land-based" game dried up and shrank, people began to look to local

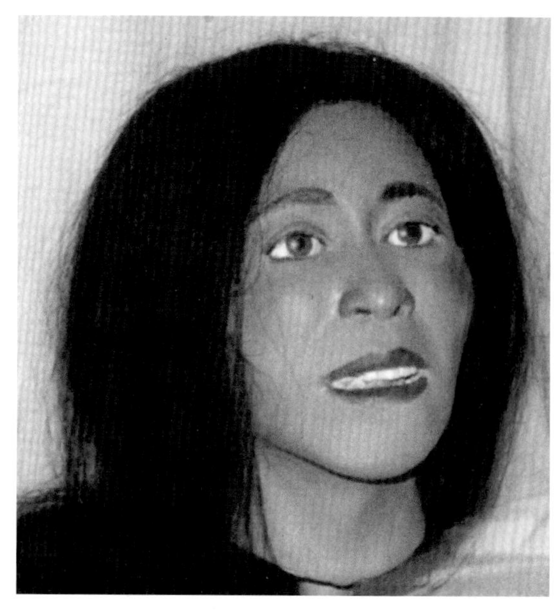

A reconstruction of the face of a Paleoindian woman buried about 10,500 years ago near Leander.

COURTESY OF THE TEXAS ARCHAEOLOGICAL RESEARCH LABORATORY, THE UNIVERSITY OF TEXAS AT AUSTIN.

streams for their food. Though most prehistoric peoples in Texas and elsewhere began to grow crops about 2,000 years ago, at the end of the Archaic period, this did not happen in central Texas. Possibly because there was an abundance of food readily available here, the inhabitants continued in their hunting-and-gathering, semi-nomadic way of life. But they did use new strategies to get and prepare their food.

During this Late Prehistoric period (from about 600 A.D. to about 1600) hunters began to use bows and arrows to kill their prey, and new projectile points were adopted. Large herds of bison returned to the area, and by about 1,000 years ago the animal had come to play an important role in the lives of people here. Archeological excavations of a large village at Rowe Valley in Williamson County found that the Indians there had established special areas to slaughter and process the bison they killed. They also ate a lot of shellfish, and large mounds of discarded shells have been found. For some reason the stone-lined earth ovens built by the Archaic people were no longer used during the Late Prehistoric period, but seeds, roots, and herbs continued to be an important part of the diet. Shards of pottery found at some central Texas sites suggest that local Indians may have traded with the Caddoan people of East Texas during this time.

It is not clear what became of the first peoples who lived in what is now Williamson County. By the early eighteenth century the Tonkawa Indians were the predominant group in the area, but they were probably unrelated to the people who had lived in the area for thousands of years before.

THE TONKAWAS IN "THE LAND OF GOOD WATER"

When the Spanish first began to travel through the area that is now Williamson County during the late 1600s and early 1700s, they found an unspoiled land filled with wildlife. As a later visitor noted, the place resembled "an English park on a grand scale." Vast expanses of waving grass, punctuated here and there by trees, supported herds of buffalo and wild horses. Deer, turkey, foxes, coyotes, and other animals were plentiful, while the area's crystal-clear creeks and rivers teemed with fish, turtles, alligators, beavers, and otters. The skies were often filled with huge flocks of birds, and, occasionally, by great swarms of bees that drifted like smoke across the horizon. As the Spanish also discovered, the area and its wildlife supported a number of Native American peoples who had grown to feel the land was their own.

In the 1700s the Tonkawa tribe dominated the Williamson County area: they called it *Takachue Pouetsu*, "The Land of Good Water." Lipan Apaches also traveled through, and after about 1800, Comanches moved into the region and began to fight the Tonkawas for control. Other Native Americans also lived in or moved through the area during the early eighteenth century. A small village of Tonkawonis is reported to have existed about fifteen miles northwest of present-day Georgetown sometime before the 1830s, and according to some sources, a small number of Kiowas also lived in the area about that time. The Double File Trail, the first defined road through the region, was created in 1828 by Delaware Indians moving from east Texas to Nuevo Laredo, Mexico.

Of the various Indian tribes who lived in or passed through the area when the Spanish arrived, the Tonkawa may have been there the longest; some evidence suggests that they moved into central Texas from the high plains in the 1600s. By the early 1700s the Tonkawas were actually a confederation of independent groups which had united at about that time. These included the original Tonkawa, who lived in the Williamson County area; the Mayeyes; and several smaller bands. In the mid-1700s the Tonkawa also absorbed the Yojuane Indians, originally a Wichita tribe. Though each of these groups probably elected its own chief, after unification the Tonkawa also picked a head chief to lead the entire tribe.

The Tonkawa way of life reflected the beliefs and customs of the Plains Indian culture that they had carried to central Texas from the north. By the seventeenth century they had acquired horses and skillfully employed their new mobility to hunt buffalo, deer, and small game. Bows and arrows (and later, guns) were used to bring down prey, and the Indians sometimes stampeded animals by setting fire to the prairie; this helped to maintain the grasslands by clearing away brush and activating the seeds of native grasses.

Buffalo meat, when it was available, was a staple of the Tonkawa diet, but when hunting was poor they ate deer, rabbit, snakes, shellfish—almost anything that was available. Though they may have planted corn or beans occasionally, the vegetable part of their diet usually consisted of wild roots, fruit, nuts, and seeds. Sometimes, when food was scarce, they were forced to go hungry. Originally the Tonkawas lived in short tepees made of buffalo hides, but when the buffalo became scarce, they built tepee-like structures out of branches and grass.

❖

Manos, knives, scrapers, perforators, and other prehistoric tools found in the 1930s by archaeologists at the J. E. Merrell site on Brushy Creek near Round Rock.

PHOTO 41WM2-27, TEXAS ARCHAEOLOGICAL RESEARCH LABORATORY, THE UNIVERSITY OF TEXAS AT AUSTIN.

Archaeology students helping to excavate a prehistoric mound near Cedar Park; the photo was taken about 1929.

PHOTO 41WM8-18, TEXAS ARCHAEOLOGICAL RESEARCH LABORATORY, THE UNIVERSITY OF TEXAS AT AUSTIN.

The Tonkawas believed in life after death and conducted elaborate funeral ceremonies. Often the deceased were buried with some of their most valued possessions; sometimes a horse would be killed and placed in the grave. Because the Tonkawas thought that spirits of the dead traveled to a home in the west, they buried bodies with the heads facing in that direction. Wolves and owls could harbor the spirit of someone not properly buried, so killing those animals was forbidden except under special circumstances. The Tonkawas also practiced ritualistic cannibalism, believing that they could ingest the best qualities of their enemies if they ate parts of their dead bodies.

The Tonkawas maintained generally good relations with the Lipan Apaches who lived in the area until the late 1700s, when the Comanches, a fierce, nomadic people unsurpassed in horseback warfare, began to move into the region from the northwest. The Tonkawas first allied themselves with the Comanches. But by the early 1800s the two tribes had become bitter enemies, and the Comanches posed a dangerous threat to the Tonkawa way of life. The tribe's population was seriously depleted by Comanche attacks and disease; in 1779 alone, a smallpox epidemic killed about half of the tribe's warriors.

By 1828, according to one description, the Tonkawas were "horse-poor," lived in crude shelters and were too fearful of the Comanches to hunt buffalo. When white settlers began to move into the area during the 1830s, the Tonkawas maintained cordial relations with the newcomers and willingly cooperated with them against their mutual enemy. The tribe signed treaties with the Republic of Texas in November 1837 and April 1838, and Tonkawas sometimes fought with the Texans against the Comanches or served as scouts. As their numbers continued to decline and white immigration increased, however, the Tonkawas completely lost control of the Williamson County area. In 1855, the tribe was removed to a reservation on the Brazos, and then, in 1859, to land in far northern Oklahoma. Several hundred members of the tribe still live there today at Fort Oakland.

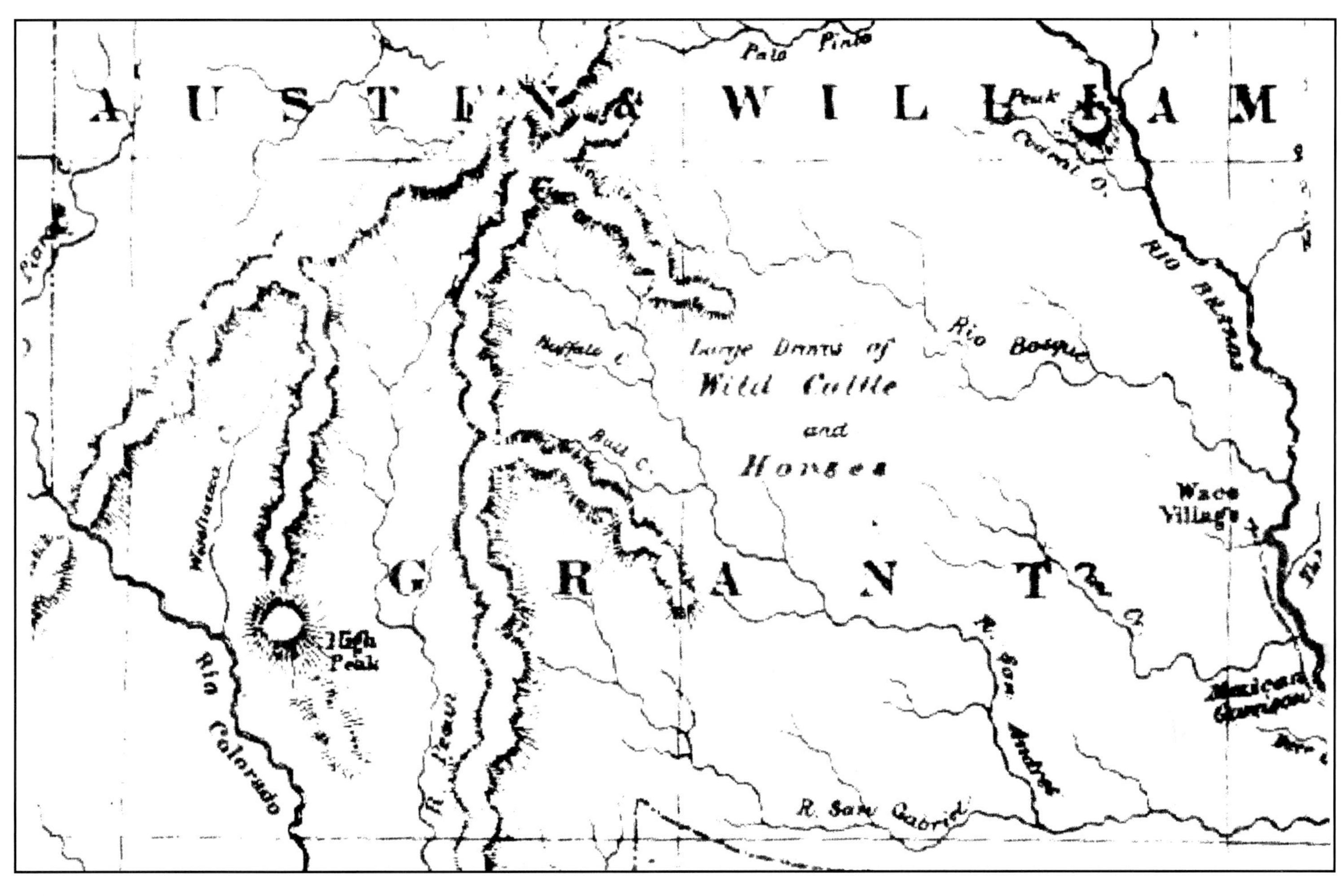

❖

A portion of Stephen F. Austin's 1837 map of Texas. The area shown includes what would later become Williamson County.

COURTESY OF TEXAS GENERAL LAND OFFICE.

Early Explorations, Missions & Land Grants

THE SPANISH

Spanish explorers probably first traversed the area that would later become Williamson County in the late 1600s, but did not become familiar with the region for a few more years. In 1716 Captain Don Domingo Ramón, escorting a number of Franciscan priests from Saltillo to Nacogdoches, was one of the first to pass through the area. The sixty-five travelers crossed Brushy Creek (naming it Arroyo de las Animas), then moved north to the San Gabriel River (calling it the San Xavier), about thirty miles west of present-day Georgetown, before turning east. In 1721 another large northbound expedition led by Governor Marqués de San Miguel de Aguayo camped on the San Xavier (San Gabriel) a few miles east of Georgetown's present site, then forded the river.

To help pacify and control the Tonkawa, Apache, and other Indians living in the area, during the late 1740s and early 1750s the Spanish established three missions and a presidio on the San Gabriel, just east of the border between present-day Williamson and Milam Counties. By July 1750 there were 480 Indians living at the missions, and 266 had been baptized into the Catholic faith. Despite some successes, the missions were plagued by problems. Apaches, sometimes traveling up the San Gabriel from the Williamson County area, attacked the missions on a number of occasions, running off horses and sometimes killing Indians and soldiers. These raids, along with drought, disease, and mismanagement, finally convinced the Spanish to abandon the missions in 1756.

Nevertheless, the Spanish continued to travel through the area. In 1761 for example, Don Felipe de Rabago y Terán journeyed along the San Gabriel, passing near present-day Georgetown, and, in 1779, the Frenchman Athanase de Mezeires, travelling in the service of the Spanish crown, noted that the region offered plenty of incentives to settlement. "Few rivers can compare with the San Xavier [San Gabriel] in the clearness of its waters or in abundance of fish," he wrote. "The surrounding country could be irrigated to avoid the uncertainty of the weather, and mills could be erected. The number of wild horses and cattle that graze here and which could be utilized as beasts of burden is incredible.... In the woods will be found, in addition to abundant game, lumber, and in the quarries, all kinds of stone for building." No Spanish land grants were ever issued for land in what is now Williamson County, though, and settlement of the area would not begin until the 1830s.

Stephen F. Austin.

COURTESY OF THE AUSTIN HISTORY CENTER.

MEXICAN LAND GRANTS

On April 15, 1825, the Mexican state of Coahuila y Tejas approved a colonization contract with Robert Leftwich, an American *empresario* from Tennessee; the huge tract opened to settlement by this agreement included present Williamson County. On August 6 of that year, Leftwich sold the rights to colonize the area to a group from Nashville, Tennessee called the Texas Association, with the stipulation that the area would thereafter be known as Leftwich's Grant. When the Mexican government reconfirmed the contract in 1827, though, it was officially granted to "the Nashville Company," after Stephen F. Austin, acting as an agent for the Texas Association, loosely translated the name of the group as "the Company from Nashville." Though Austin was supposed to be negotiating with the Mexican government on behalf of the interests of Sterling Clack Robertson and other stockholders of the Nashville group, he later applied to the government for the area himself; and, in February 1831, the contract for the area was awarded to Austin and his secretary, Samuel May Williams. Between 1831 and 1834, when the area was known as Austin's "upper colony," the first six land grants in the Williamson County area were issued. Two small grants in the southern part of the region went to Jacob Ebberly and Jacob Casner in 1832; and in 1833 four huge eleven-league grants that included lands in the northern part of the Williamson area (each league contained 4,428 acres) were awarded to Jose Justo Liendo, Pedro Zarza, Miguel Davila, and Miguel de Aguirre. Apparently none of these people actually settled on their Williamson properties. Their heirs later sold some of the land, and much of the property in the eleven-league parcels was later granted to others.

In 1834 the Austin and Williams contract with respect to the Nashville Colony was cancelled, a new contract was awarded to Sterling Clack Robertson, and the area became known as "Robertson's Colony." In 1835 ten tracts in what is now Williamson County were granted by the Mexican government under the terms of Robertson's contract; the second of these, a one-league tract granted August 10, 1835 to one Orvill Perry, included part of present-day Georgetown. Another league, granted to Elijah Harmon, encompassed part of what is now Leander. Just north of Harmon's land, another league was granted to noted pioneer Greenleaf Fisk, who moved to the area a few years later.

By the beginning of the Texas Revolution in 1835, the Williamson County area remained almost entirely controlled by the Tonkawa, Comanche and other Indians who lived or roamed in the region, but within a few years hundreds of Anglo-American settlers would move in, putting down roots and bringing the area within the orbit of the new Republic of Texas.

❖

Berry's Mill, established in 1848 on Berry's Creek northwest of Georgetown, was the first mill built in the county. It is not known when this photo was taken, but under magnification John and Hannah Berry, and seven of their children, can be seen standing on the left.

COURTESY OF THE WILLIAMSON COUNTY HISTORICAL COMMISSION AND JACK POPE.

Early Settlement in Williamson County

1835-1848

The colonization efforts of Stephen F. Austin and other *empresarios* had attracted many Anglo-Americans to settlements just east and south of the Williamson County area, and as these people became more familiar with the region, settlers began to filter into the Tonkawa's "Land of Good Water." Captain Cal Putnam, who constructed a blockhouse near present-day Liberty Hill in the early 1830s, was one of the first Anglo-Americans to move into the region. By the mid-1830s, more and more hunters, land agents, and Indian fighters from settlements to the south and east were traveling through. Though the threat of Indian attack deterred settlement for several years, by 1835 land surveyors were already laying out tracts along the San Gabriel River. It was dangerous work: two surveyors were killed along the San Gabriel by Indians in late 1835, and another was killed near Brushy Creek the next year.

To help protect frontier areas, in late 1835 the newly-established Provisional Government of Texas created three companies of Rangers and ordered a fort built on the western reaches of Brushy Creek. In January of the next year, Captain John Tumlinson led sixty men to a site about four miles south of the center of present-day Leander, and built a blockhouse and stockade; a lookout post in a huge oak tree gave them a sweeping view of the surrounding countryside. Tumlinson's Fort, as the outpost came to be known, was abandoned in March 1836 when the Ranger company was withdrawn but its creation had been a sign of the growing interest in the region. Though Indians burned the fort not long after the Rangers left, the lookout tree lived on into the 1960s. By 1985 it had been cut down, and the site is now part of a housing development.

The new Republic of Texas offered generous land grants to new settlers, Revolutionary veterans, and others. Thousands of immigrants traveled to Texas in the aftermath of the Texas Revolution, and many Texans from older, more established settlements also began to look west for new lands. As the demand for land intensified, the frontier moved westward. Texas Rangers attacked Indian

George Washington Glasscock (1810-1879). This photo is from Williamson County, Texas: Its History and Its People.

COURTESY OF HAZEL HOOD.

tribes in central Texas and elsewhere to push them out of the path of the pioneers and to ensure the safety of existing settlements. Meanwhile the Mexican government apparently encouraged Indian attacks; Mexico had not yet resigned itself to the loss of Texas and hoped to destabilize the new Republic. In May 1839, about nine miles west of present-day Georgetown, a company of Texas Rangers led by James Rice attacked a group of Mexicans and Indians in what has become known as the Battle of the San Gabriels. A few months later, a group of more than eighty Rangers engaged about 100 Comanches in a bloody battle a few miles south of present-day Taylor.

During the late 1830s and early 1840s, as the demand for Texas lands intensified, a number of small settlements were established in western Milam County, which included what would soon become Williamson County. Dr. Thomas Kenney established what was probably the first permanent settlement in the area. Kenney, born in Kentucky in 1805, had fought in the Black Hawk War in Illinois before moving to Stephen F. Austin's colony in 1833, and had served as a surgeon during the Texas Revolution. In 1839—the same year Austin was established as the capital of Texas—Kenney moved his wife and three daughters from Bastrop to a fort he and others had built in 1838 where the Double File Trail crossed Brushy Creek, just south of present-day Palm Valley.

Kenney's Fort, as the settlement came to be known, was a half-acre square enclosure defined by four log cabins, each on a corner of the fort, linked by tall wooden fences. Portholes in the cabin walls made the place easier to defend, and gates on the west and east sides were big enough to allow large covered wagons to enter. About fifteen to twenty people, including Texas Rangers James Rice and Joseph Weeks, lived at the fort. At least three women, including Mrs. Kenney and Mrs. Weeks, lived with their husbands there, but the pioneers at the fort were mostly men; as Dr. Kenney's daughter Mary Jane later remembered, the place "was home for every idle and homeless man my father could find." The settlers provided for themselves by planting corn and hunting buffalo and other game for food and hides. Meanwhile others, like George Washington Glasscock, were already preparing to follow the line of settlement further.

Glasscock, born in Kentucky, had once been a partner with Abraham Lincoln on an Illinois flatboat. He had moved to Texas in 1835, and by 1838—when Kenney's Fort was being built—he was in Bastrop working with two partners in a wide-ranging land speculation operation. In June 1838, Glasscock wrote his brother about his recent trip up the San Gabriel River, and enthusiastically described the land he had seen as "the finest watered part of Texas that I have seen [with] fine springs limestone water and rock and soil as good as any in Texas...a splendid piece of land as I ever saw." Glasscock had already purchased four leagues of land in the area, but since he understood the dangers of

life on the frontier, he planned to stay in Bastrop until "the Sant Gabrels is settled."

Others, less cautious and unwilling to wait, continued to move into the area, with sometimes disastrous results. In 1839 John Webster led a group of sixteen men, women and children toward land he had bought in what is now eastern Burnet County. Not long after their wagons had crossed the south fork of the San Gabriel the group spotted a band of Comanches and turned back south. When they arrived at Brushy Creek at sunrise the Comanches attacked. In the desperate fight that followed all of the Webster party's fourteen men were killed; Webster's wife and children survived but were captured by the Indians. At about this same time, one or two other families who tried to settle along the San Gabriel east of Georgetown were forced to leave because of Indian attacks.

The settlers' relations with the local Indians were not always unfriendly. The Tonkawas, seeking allies against their hated enemies, the Comanches, sometimes served as scouts in Ranger raids, and gave settlers food and advice. Dr. Kenney's daughter, Mary Jane, later remembered often seeing at Kenney's Fort "thirty and forty Indians in that court[yard] eating food which Dr. Kenney had prepared for them. He was unusually kind to them." But the Comanches were unrelentingly hostile. Kenney's Fort was attacked in 1840, and the threat of raids and ambushes continued for years thereafter. In April 1844, Dr. Kenney and two companions were attacked by Comanches while they were hunting buffalo north of the San Gabriel. All three men were killed and scalped.

For several years Kenney's Fort was the center of settler activity along Brushy Creek, and travelers through the area often stopped there. In June 1841 about 320 armed Texans assembled near Kenney's Fort, at what they called Camp Cazneau. There they prepared to embark on what has become known as the Santa Fe Expedition, an attempt by President Mirabeau Lamar to establish Texas' claim to Santa Fe. After Lamar visited the camp to encourage them, the men set out in high spirits along the Double File Trail, marching to music. Hunting buffalo, fishing, and shooting alligators for sport, the expeditioners camped on the San Gabriel near present-day Weir the first night, and on the second on Possum Creek. The good times didn't last long. When the remnants of the expedition finally straggled into Santa Fe almost four months later, the Mexican authorities had no trouble arresting the Texans, and they were taken to Mexico City and imprisoned.

Kenney's Fort also played a role in the so-called Archives War. In 1842 the Mexican government responded to the Santa Fe fiasco by sending an army to capture San Antonio. Many settlers in the area surrounding Austin, in fear for their lives, abandoned their homes. Meanwhile President Sam Houston—who had never liked moving the capital to Austin in the first place—changed the capital to Washington-on-the-Brazos, and ordered that the Republic's land records be moved there too. Austin residents keenly resented the move, which would have been a real blow to Austin's prospects for growth and prosperity. One man wrote to Houston: "We did heare that you was

The Smart-McCormick House, located about eight miles northwest of Andice, was built by slaves in the 1850s. Its original owner, Bryce Miller Smart, moved to the Gabriel Mills area in 1851 and operated a freight line to Brenham.

COURTESY OF THE WILLIAMSON COUNTY HISTORICAL COMMISSION AND MADGE MCCORMICK SMITH.

goin move the seat of government and the publik papers.... You Dam old drunk Cherokee." Nevertheless, on December 30, twenty soldiers left Austin with three wagonloads of land records. That night, en route to the new capital, they stopped at Kenney's Fort. Just behind them was a group of enraged Austinites, who, armed with a cannon, surrounded the fort and demanded the records be returned. The farce ended peacefully with the papers back in Austin.

Soon after Kenney's Fort had been established, other Anglo-Americans had begun moving into the surrounding countryside. In 1838 or 1839, Adam Lawrence, who had come to Texas in 1822 as part of Stephen Austin's colony, settled with his wife, Sarah, and their family in a log cabin on the Brushy about ten miles southeast of present-day Taylor; in 1840 he donated land for a cemetery there, and the place came to be known as Lawrence Chapel. The Olive family's long trek from Mississippi ended near the Brushy in 1843, when James Olive bought land from Lawrence, built a cabin, and, soon afterward, a store in Lawrence Chapel. That same year Washington Anderson, originally from Virginia and a hero of the Battle of San Jacinto, bought the John Wiley tract (which now contains most of Round Rock's "historic district") and settled there with his wife, Mary, and their children; soon thereafter he built one of the first gristmills in the county. By this time stagecoaches were already running through Post Oak Island, an "island" of post oaks on the prairie southwest of Lawrence Chapel. It would soon become the stage stop for the surrounding area.

As the Brushy Creek area filled in during the 1840s, others began to settle in the rolling sections north and west. John Berry, originally from Kentucky, had fought in the Battle of Tippecanoe during the War of 1812 and had moved to Illinois and then Indiana before arriving in Texas in 1827. Three of his sons served in the Texas Revolution. In 1846, Berry settled his family on what is now known as Berry's Creek, about three miles northeast of present-day Georgetown, and, in 1848, constructed a gristmill. "They come from far and near to see my mill spring, to see this great fountain of water boiling out of the earth," Berry wrote a relative. "...This land is the best farming land I have ever seen. The country is pleasant and healthful." At about this same time, Greenleaf Fisk settled with his family and slaves on his league on the South San Gabriel. Many others would soon follow.

Jane and Silas Vickers of Liberty Hilol. Silas moved to Texas in 1845 from Ohio. Jane moved in 1848 from Mississippi. They married in Caldwell County and then moved to Williamson; they had fourteen children together.

COURTESY OF THE WILLIAMSON COUNTY HISTORICAL COMMISSION AND LOLA KING.

The first Williamson County Courthouse, used between 1849 and May 1851.

COURTESY OF THE WILLIAMSON COUNTY HISTORICAL COMMISSION AND MUSEUM.

The Creation of Williamson County

1848-1860

Settlement in the area intensified during the late 1840s after Texas was annexed by the United States. While most of the early settlers were originally from the southern United States, many were not. In 1846 and 1847, for example, several families, including the Makemsons, the Smalleys, and the Knights, migrated from Vermillion County, Illinois, and established themselves around Brushy Creek. As the area filled in, businesses and social institutions began to emerge.

The first post office was created at "Brushy," possibly located on what is now the Southwestern University golf course, in 1847. In 1848, about the same time that John Berry built his mill, George Washington Glasscock built another mill on the San Gabriel just east of present-day San Gabriel Park; Jacob Harrell moved from Austin to establish a blacksmith shop on Brushy Creek where Round Rock is today; and Nelson Morey set up a general store on the Brushy south of present-day Hutto. That same year the area's first Baptist congregation, the Missionary Baptist Church, was organized in a log cabin about a mile north of Brushy Creek in present-day Round Rock, and a log school also began to operate nearby. Soon afterward, Samuel Makemson helped to establish another school in the Brushy Creek area.

At least 250 people were living in the region by this time, and as the population rapidly increased local citizens organized to form their own government. Washington Anderson and James Rice circulated a petition asking the Texas legislature, "as an act of convenience and justice," to create a new county. "Your petitioners would...represent to your Hon. body that in their present situation it is very inconvenient for them to attend the courts of Milam County, most of them having to go from 40 to 50 miles," the document read. By February 1848, when the petition was submitted, 107 people had signed, and on March 13, 1848 the state legislature created the new county. Although the petitioners had requested that it be named "Clear Water County," or "San Gabriel County," the legislature named the new jurisdiction after a popular state senator, Judge Robert McAlpin Williamson. "Three-Legged Willie," as Williamson was called, never lived within the bounds of the new county, but his judicial circuit had once included the area, and he was as well-known for his courage and oratorical skills as he was for the wooden peg he kept strapped to the knee of his shriveled right leg.

In May 1848, George Washington Glasscock and his partner Thomas Huling donated 173 acres near the confluence of the North and South San Gabriels for the county's seat of government. In return for the donation, it was agreed that new town would be called "Georgetown" in Glasscock's honor. The first county court was convened under a huge oak tree on the site, but within a few months a small log courthouse had been built to conduct business; the first jail was simply a wooden wagon turned upside down.

For several years Georgetown remained a crude village "with almost limitless prairies stretching away on every side." It offered only the most rudimentary comforts to its few inhabitants and visitors. During the early 1850s, the place consisted mainly of a few log houses, the courthouse, a jail, a few stores and a hotel, all loosely connected by dirt paths that with rain quickly turned to mud. According to one story, Circuit Judge Robert Jones Rivers was staying in Georgetown's Ake Hotel in 1854 when he caught pneumonia. Informed by Parson Stephen Strickland that he was facing death, and aware of the "desolate and depressing scene" outside his window, Rivers reportedly replied, "Parson.... I have been a great traveler in my day and time—have visited Europe...stopped in magnificent hotels, lodged in inns and taverns, and I tell you now, Parson...I know of no place that I can quit with fewer regrets than the new city of Georgetown and particularly this Ake Hotel." With that, he "turned his face to the wall" and died.

Thousands of new settlers moved to the area soon after the county was organized; Williamson's population rose to 1,568 by 1850 and to 4,524 by 1860. Some established farms on the flat, fertile blackland prairie in the eastern and southern sections of the county, supporting fledgling communities like Rice's Crossing (created about 1849), Brushy (later called Round Rock, 1851), Circleville (1853), Shiloh (1854), Post Oak Island (1855), and Macedonia (1855). Many others moved to the more rugged western part of the county, where wood and limestone for building were readily available, and

The remnants of a stone wall built by slaves who cleared this field near Florence in the 1850s.

COURTESY OF JOHN J. LEFFLER.

villages such as Gabriel Mills (1849), Bagdad (1854), Liberty Hill (1854), Florence (1857), Andice (1857), and Pleasant Hill (1857) began to grow. There had been only one post office in Williamson when the county was created in 1848. But, by 1860, there were thirteen, and schools and churches were being built all around the area. Meanwhile Masonic lodges, centers of civic and social activities, were established in Georgetown (1851), Gabriel Mills (1853), Post Oak Island (1855) and Round Rock (1858).

As the population grew, Williamson County's economy also evolved and matured. Tens of thousands of wild longhorn steers still roamed the range, and many settlers still hunted them for hides and meat. By 1860 many stockmen in the area were raising domesticated cattle and sheep. The U.S. Census counted almost 53,000 cattle, including almost 15,000 milk cows, on the 356 farms and ranches in Williamson that year, and the county's 17,000 sheep produced almost 33,000 pounds of wool. Meanwhile thousands of acres were being cultivated to grow corn, wheat, oats, and other crops. A few farmers began growing cotton in the early 1850s. The county's first cotton gin was established at Rice's Crossing in 1852, and the bales were hauled south to Bastrop in ox-drawn wagons for sale. In 1860 cotton was still a minor crop in the area, though, and only 271 bales were produced that year.

While Williamson County's economy was rapidly developing, the settlers still lived under conditions their eastern cousins would have considered crude, harsh, and dangerous. Most families still lived crowded into simple one- or two-room log cabins with sometimes nothing but packed dirt for a floor. Most homes were sparsely furnished, containing little more than bedsteads, a table, and chairs. Except for pieces carried into the area by wagon, almost all the furniture was hand-made; homespun cloth and deerhides provided material for clothes. Glass panes were extremely rare, and during the winter when the windows were shuttered against the cold, the dwellings were dark and gloomy, with only primitive oil lamps or tallow candles for light. Fireplaces provided both living heat and a place to cook, but also danger: the mud-and-wattle chimneys built by some of the settlers were prone to fires that could, and sometimes did, spread to the rest of the cabin.

Life was filled with uncertainty. While the settlers often effectively used native herbs for various ailments, doctors were few and far between, and in any case medical science was quite primitive. The Williamson County area had a reputation as a healthy place to live, but epidemics of smallpox, typhoid and other diseases sometimes decimated families. Childbirth was an experience always fraught with danger for both mother and child, and the many infant graves in local cemeteries still attest that infant mortality rates were high. Though the Indian threat was much reduced, Comanches raided into the area as late as the 1860s.

Farmers also had to live with unpredictable rainfall and uncontrollable pests, which sometimes devastated local crops. In a letter to his brother in 1858, Samuel Carothers, who lived in the southwestern reaches of the county, described a recent locust attack: "The grasshoppers come up from the south near the Gulf where they hatch. They come upon us on 7th May from the south & southeast in swarms about 11 o'clock, then air

Mrs. C. C. Langford sitting at her "old-time loom," the type used by early settlers in Williamson County. This photo was quite possibly taken at a reunion of the Williamson County Old Settlers Association during the early 1900s. Note Mrs. Langford's "pioneer" attire and the tents and covered wagons in the background.

PHOTO IV-0547, GEORGETOWN HERITAGE SOCIETY.

and sun darkened [as the locusts were] passing over and dropping down thick as flakes of snow all over the face of the county and [they] went to work and in a few hours every blade of wheat and corn and everything that they could eat was devoured...it is not in my power to describe them and my feelings, I can't do it. It looked like one of Pharos Plagues as I have imagined it."

Religion and music helped many of the early settlers to cope with the trials of frontier life, while other activities, like gambling and horseracing, also provided some diversion. A racetrack was established on the northeastern side of Georgetown by 1850, and the intensity of the competition there can be seen in a gambling contract drawn up that year. G. M. Williams agreed to race his gray stallion, *Buttons*, against *Blue Dick*, Alfred Bailes' horse, at Georgetown's quarter-mile track on the first Thursday of November. The stakes: one thousand dollars, a huge sum at the time.

Most of the people who moved into Williamson County before the Civil War had been born in Texas or in other southern states like Tennessee, Kentucky, Arkansas, Missouri, and South Carolina, and a number brought slaves with them. By 1860 there were 891 slaves in the county, almost twenty percent of the county's total population. They were put to work clearing rocks from fields, building houses, barns, and fences, and tending crops and livestock. As Harry Chrisman writes in his book *The Ladder of Rivers*, slaves in Williamson County, like other southern slaves, were kept "subjugated, segregated, uneducated, and... dependent on their masters." In 1853, as the number of slaves in the area increased, the County Court organized a slave patrol in Georgetown to deter runaways and to guard against the possibility of a slave rebellion. By the late 1850s similar patrols had been established in Round Rock, Florence, and three other communities. There were no large plantations in the county, however, and this may have led to more personal relationships between the county's slaves and their masters than might otherwise have been the case.

Some slaves in the county, like Austin Smith, managed to use their talents and energies to carve out opportunities within the "peculiar institution." Smith, one of a group of slaves brought into the area from Arkansas during the 1840s, was widely regarded for his stonemasonry, and his master allowed him to hire himself out to the owners of surrounding farms. Within a few years he had saved enough money to buy his own land in the Lewis Dyches survey. Unlike the situation in some parts of the Old South, there were very few free blacks in the county. James Olive, who had a stock farm near Brushy Creek, owned one slave named Lars, and also employed two free blacks, "Uncle" Arnos and "Aunt" Phoebe Kelley. But the U.S. Census counted only three free blacks in Williamson County in 1850, and none at all by 1860.

While slavery was legally protected and generally accepted by the white citizens of the county during this time, a number of whites sympathized with the slaves, and some even worked actively to undermine the institution. In 1853, Freeman Smalley, a minister born in New York, established the Anti-Slaveholding Union Baptist Church a couple miles east of Round Rock; it was the first of its kind in Texas. And according to tradition, the prominent Georgetown resident Elias Talbot secretly helped slaves to escape and occasionally hid runaways in a tunnel beneath his house.

Though still close to the edge of the Texas western frontier, by 1860 Williamson County was rapidly filling up and and developing into a settled and stable area. The beginning of the Civil War in 1861, however, would lead to events that seriously disrupted the area's economy and transformed its social relations.

❖

John and Fannie Robinson helped establish the African Methodist Episcopal Church in Taylor in the 1870s.

COURTESY OF THE WILLIAMSON COUNTY HISTORICAL COMMISSION AND LESLIE HILL.

THE CIVIL WAR & RECONSTRUCTION

Secession fever began to sweep across the South after Abraham Lincoln was elected president in 1860. South Carolina left the Union first, in December 1860, followed by Alabama, Mississippi, Florida, Georgia, and Louisiana. Meanwhile, Texans hotly debated whether to follow suit. Texas Governor Sam Houston, a strong believer in the sanctity of the Union, opposed the secession movement and toured the state thundering against it. As part of his effort to hold back the tide, he traveled to Williamson County to confer with known Unionists in Georgetown and to address crowds assembled in what is now San Gabriel Park.

Ultimately, of course, Houston lost the battle, and in an election held in February 1861, Texans voted 46,129 to 14,697 to take their state out of the Union. Secession was overwhelmingly popular in eastern Texas, where slavery was a central fact of life, but many people living in south Texas and along the frontier opposed secession. In Williamson County, the relatively small number of slaveholders, and the influence of men like Freeman Smalley and Elias Talbot, help to explain hostility to the measure. Of the state's 122 counties, Williamson was one of only eighteen that stood against secession; in the February election the county's citizens voted 480 to 349 to stay in the Union.

The divisions reflected in that vote persisted during the long Civil War that followed. A number of Williamson County men simply refused to fight for the Confederacy and went to Mexico to avoid conscription and harassment. Animosities between ardent Confederates and known (or suspected) Union sympathizers occasionally led to violence and sometimes even murder. The most vicious incident involving the county occurred in July 1863, when eight Williamson men on their way to Mexico were captured by Confederate soldiers near Bandera, about fifty miles northwest of San Antonio. Although some of the men had served in the Texas militia, the Confederates hanged them without trial, then stripped the bodies and took whatever valuables they could find.

Despite these divisions, most men and women in the county, including some of those who had voted against secession, loyally supported the Confederate cause after the war had begun. Five companies of troops were raised in Williamson County, including a "spy" company led by James Rice, a Texas Ranger detachment, and three companies of cavalry (almost all the men supplied their own horses). Men from the county also enlisted in other companies organized in the surrounding area.

Williamson County recruits fought in some of most vicious battles of that particularly vicious war. I. P. "Print" Olive, for example, served in the Second Texas Infantry regiment, which lost more than a third of its men at the Battle of Shiloh in April 1862; by the following November, the regiment had been reduced to 250 of its original 1,300 men. Wounded at least once, Olive was finally sent home after being captured during the grueling siege of Vicksburg. Another aspect of the war's brutality was described by John Mankins, who had to leave his wife Betty and his child behind in Williamson County when he enlisted. In March 1863, he wrote Betty that he had just seen two Texans shot for desertion: "They shuck hands and kissed and then knelt on their knees and was boath shot dead." It was, Mankins wrote, a sight "I never want to witness again." Like Mankins, who died later in the war, a number of Williamson soldiers never returned, and those who did would never be quite the same.

A tintype of Williamson County pioneer Daniel Harrison (1816-1870) who first moved to Texas in the 1830s and fought at the Battle of San Jacinto and in the Civil War.

COURTESY OF THE WILLIAMSON COUNTY HISTORICAL COMMISSION AND MARY HODGE.

While the war caused many young men to leave the county, at least for the duration of the conflict, it also led to an increase in the area's slave population as southerners fled into Texas to escape the Union threat. William Clark, for example, left Tennessee with his family and slaves after the war broke out. Hauling their possessions in oxcarts, the Clarks took six weeks to reach central Texas; Clark then traded two of his slaves for a farm near Round Rock. By 1864, according to county tax records, there were 1,074 slaves in Williamson County.

Though no battles were ever fought anywhere near Williamson County, the war required difficult sacrifices even from those who stayed behind. Men and women on the homefront often did what they could to promote the war effort and to help out their "boys" in the lines by donating items like clothes, food, cotton, and livestock to the Confederate cause. Many women like Betty Mankins had to struggle to work their lands without the help of their husbands and sons, and lived in dread of bad news from the front. So many families were impoverished that the county government occasionally distributed medicine, cloth and other items to help them get through the war. Hired help was hard to find; and in any case, money was in short supply, as were "luxuries" like coffee. Since the departure of so many men left the settlements more vulnerable, Indian attacks intensified during the war years. In August 1863, Comanches raiding into the southwestern corner of the county killed Wofford Johnson and his wife and youngest daughter. The Johnsons were the last settlers killed by Indians in Williamson County.

The gravestone of William Bacon Tucker in the Rocky Hollow Cemetery. According to tradition Tucker, who served in the Confederate ranks during the Civil War, was walking back to his home in Williamson County in 1865, but decided at the spot where his grave marker now stands that he could go no further. He died under the old oak tree that now shades his grave.

COURTESY OF JOHN J. LEFFLER.

The Civil War and its aftermath seriously disrupted the area's economy and transformed its social relations. On June 19, 1865, as some of Williamson County's defeated Confederate veterans were still walking home from the war, Union General Gordon Granger landed in Galveston and officially proclaimed the end of slavery in Texas. As Williamson's ex-slaves rejoiced in their freedom, everyone in the area began to adjust to the many implications of the new, still undefined social order.

For the freedmen, emancipation meant both opportunity and uncertainty. They now were free to leave; but without money or property, how would they support themselves and their families? In the months and years that followed, many did leave the area: in 1870, the Census counted 801 blacks in the county, a drop of about twenty percent from 1864. Many freedmen, however, chose to remain in Williamson County, either working for small wages or as sharecroppers. Some managed to buy land, or established themselves as independent farmers on acreage given to them by their former masters or sympathetic whites.

In the process, the county's freedmen created a number of small communities, mostly in the western part of the county. Not long after emancipation, for example, Milas, Nelson, and Richard Miller bought property in the John Jenks survey, near present-day Liberty Hill. The Millers built an arbor for religious services and encouraged other freedmen to move into the vicinity; a school and rock church were eventually constructed, and the black community known as Jenks Branch or Liberty Chapel emerged. Austin Smith settled on the land he had bought while still a slave, and his holdings later became the nucleus of a community known as Stump Toe, or Rocky Hollow.

Another freedman community was created by Harry Bailey, who traded a horse and saddle for some acreage a few miles east of Georgetown and sold land to other African-Americans. After Bailey donated a piece of land, the people worked together to construct a building that served as a church and school. In the late 1860s a freedman community called Liberia also existed, but its location is not known. Blacks in the county also began to create their own social institutions: in 1869, a missionary for the African Methodist Episcopal Church, the Reverend Richard R. Haywood, established Georgetown's first black congregation. Despite their new freedom, the ex-slaves still had to contend with the racial prejudice that had long been engrained in American society. The editor of the *Georgetown Watchman* echoed the views of most whites in the county when in 1870 he derided the concept of equal rights for the freedman: "We favor white supremacy, white officers, white juries, white schools, [and] separate tables and seats and public houses for Caucasians and Ethiopians."

Meanwhile Williamson County's whites worked to come to terms with economic problems the war had created. The end of slavery had left some of the county's farmers without labor to work their fields, and they had little or no money to hire help; often they resorted to letting their lands out to freedmen sharecroppers. But the former slaves and slaveholders were by no means alone in their economic straits: Williamson's entire agricultural economy had been severely strained by the demands of the Civil War.

Thousands of acres which had been "improved" by 1860 had been abandoned during the war because there were not enough men to work them. As late as 1870, five years after the war was over, only 18,000 acres in the county were classified as improved, almost fifteen percent fewer than in 1860. Farmland in the county was worth less than half of what it had been when the war began. The county's domesticated livestock had also been seriously depleted during the war: in 1870, there were about twenty-five percent fewer horses, mules, and sheep in the county than in 1860. As late as 1876, the county government was deeply in debt, and its warrants were selling at thirty cents to the dollar. While by the early 1870s some of the area's ranchmen already had begun to raise fortunes driving cattle to markets in the North, the county's economy would not

Sam Bass, seated center, was a ne'er-do-well turned train robber. He was fatally wounded by Texas Rangers in Round Rock on July 19, 1878 after shooting two Williamson County deputies who challenged his violation of Round Rock's gun control laws. To the right is Jim Murphy, a member of the Bass gang, who informed the Rangers about the gang's whereabouts in return for clemency.

COURTESY OF AUSTIN HISTORY CENTER.

recover completely from the Civil War until many years after the conflict had ended.

While Williamson citizens struggled with economic problems during the late 1860s and early 1870s, the county was also torn by political animosities and lawlessness that grew out of the war. Before Texas was readmitted to the Union in 1870, the state was occupied by Union troops, and for most of this Reconstruction period, it was ruled by the federal government as part of the Fifth Military District. Old Unionists in Williamson County, as in other parts of Texas, looked to the federals for protection, and tended to drift into the Republican Party. The resentment of ex-Confederates sometimes boiled into violence. In the summer of 1865, for example, several men were arrested in the county for committing "flagrant crimes" and the "illegal persecution of Union men."

Many of the county's most influential citizens worked to reduce these tensions, to bury old resentments and find middle ground. A "reconciliation meeting" was held in the county in September 1865, and William Makemson, the Republican editor of the *Georgetown Watchman*, repeatedly called for harmony. "No feelings, political, sectional, or sectarian should have a place in our hearts," he wrote in August 1867. "[O]ld differences should be forgiven and forgotten, and brotherly love prevail.... That which has passed cannot be recalled." Williamson County's interests would be served best, Makemson thought, if people could put politics aside and focus on rebuilding the area's economy. He could not help but note, though, that a few "substantial men" were organizing against him and the other Republicans in the county. By 1868, over 100 men had joined the "Georgetown Democratic Club," the "Round Rock Democratic Club" had thirty-one members, and the "Florence Democratic Club" had fifty-two. By 1869, the county's government was back in the hands of conservative Democrats.

For several years after the war, the southern part of the county was particularly troubled by gangs of rootless, often violent deserters, ex-soldiers, and criminals who seem to have roamed the area almost at will, stealing cattle, horses, and money. According to an Austin newspaper, it was unsafe to ride through parts of Williamson and Lee Counties without being "well-armed." Though some of these men may have been ex-Confederates who targeted old Unionists and Republicans, virtually no one was safe from crime; people in the Round Rock area were particularly harassed by midnight raids. Dr. John C. Black of Round Rock, who attempted to stand up to the gangs, was assassinated in 1870, leading the editor of the *Watchman* to complain bitterly that the county was "teeming with criminals." "[S]o long as this continues," he wrote, "we know not who will be the next victim—probably your editor, some high official...or a good citizen. Is there no recourse? Will...our people quietly hold their hands in timid submission to the human devils that surround them??" The area continued to be plagued by banditry and violence well into the 1870s. Residents of Round Rock and Georgetown came to know the infamous killer John Wesley Hardin by sight—he lived in each town for a while—and Sam Bass was killed in Round Rock in 1878.

❖

Williamson County's fourth courthouse, built from 1877-1878. The county jail can be seen at left. The man with the horse is William Oscar Stubblefield.

COURTESY OF THE WILLIAMSON COUNTY HISTORICAL COMMISSION AND BILLY RAY STUBBLEFIELD.

Cowboys & Colleges

WILLIAMSON COUNTY IN TRANSITION

During the late 1860s Williamson County entered the era of the great cattle drives, which lasted until the early 1880s. Texans had driven herds of longhorns to Louisiana, Missouri, and Kansas before the Civil War, and the Confederates had organized drives during the war itself to procure beef for their soldiers. After the war, however, demand for Texas cattle expanded exponentially as northerners developed an appetite for beef and vast new ranching enterprises were created on the Great Plains.

Wild longhorn cattle had multiplied rapidly during the Civil War years, and by the late 1860s there were many thousands of them roaming the open ranges and brushy thickets of Williamson County: in 1866 one rancher alone counted over 4,000 unbranded longhorns in the vicinity of his home south of Brushy Creek. Averaging from 1,000 to 1,400 pounds, the huge animals "ranged in colors like the spectrum of the rainbow," their six-foot horns twisted in almost every imaginable configuration. With the post-war demand for cattle in the north, the longhorns represented wealth on the hoof for anybody who could catch and herd them. Excellent profits could also be made driving domesticated cattle. By the early 1870s, cattle bought in Texas for five to ten dollars a head could bring $20 to $25 dollars each in Kansas City, for a gross profit of $45,000 for a herd of 3,000 animals. At that time, the average American worker earned less than $300 per year.

Beginning in 1867, cattle were driven from south Texas across Williamson County along a number of different routes that, further north, fed into the famous Chisholm Trail. One trail entered the southeastern corner of the county and traveled north across the prairie; another crossed Brushy Creek at Round Rock, heading north (roughly following the path of present-day Interstate 35) to Georgetown, where the cattle forded the San Gabriel River near what is now San Gabriel Park.

Cattlemen began to conduct massive cow hunts in Williamson County soon after the end of the war. In August 1867, R. M. Overstreet, A. J. Hanna, and one Mr. Julin organized the first cattle drive from the county, taking a herd north from Brushy Creek to Abilene, Kansas. By the early 1870s a number of other local cattlemen were collecting herds and driving them to railroad heads and ranches in Colorado, Kansas, Montana, Nebraska, Nevada, and Wyoming. The cattle drives, whether just passing through Williamson or organized by men in the county, added a dramatic new element to the area's culture and its sense of identity; thanks partly to the cattle drives, the area came to have a more "western" feel than other counties to the east. By the 1870s virtually every town had its own cattle pens, and saloons in Georgetown and Round Rock catered to the tastes of the cowboys passing through.

A sizeable crowd assembled in 1898 to watch the laying the cornerstone for Southwestern University's new main building (now called the Cullen Building).

COURTESY OF THE GEORGETOWN HERITAGE SOCIETY.

Perhaps the largest cattle outfits in the county were run by Thomas and Dudley Snyder, whose land included the area occupied now by Southwestern University, and by the Olive family, who had their pens just south of present-day Thrall. But over the years probably hundreds of men in the county, white, black, and tejano, worked in the cattle hunts and either conducted drives themselves or participated in them. It was hard, sometimes dangerous work that demanded skill and stamina. One cattleman recalled the suffering endured by his men in April 1879 while driving a herd through Williamson County: "A rain, a terrible rain, came up about four o'clock in the evening, raining all evening and all night. It was very cold and we came near to freezing to death.... Cattle drifted before wind-driven rain, and by morning we were at Hutto, eight miles away; we had no supper and no breakfast, and not till noon did we have anything to eat."

The cattle bonanza, which created jobs and generated many thousands of dollars for local ranchers and merchants, did much to alleviate the county's postwar economic problems. As early as April 1870, the *Watchman* commented on the area's "unprecedented prosperity, which has been brought about by the exertions of a small proportion of our citizens." Meanwhile,

the people of Williamson were beginning to create new institutions to build, refine, and inform local society.

When a group called the Young Men's Debating and Literary Society was organized in Liberty Hill in 1867, the editor of the *Watchman* called for a similar club in Georgetown. Others worked to rid their communities of the pernicious effects of alcohol: reform-minded citizens of Georgetown organized a local Council of the Friends of Temperance in 1870, and by April of that year it had forty-seven members. Meanwhile a large

Newton Calvin Holman setting out on a cattle drive from Williamson County in 1883.

COURTESY OF THE WILLIAMSON COUNTY HISTORICAL COMMISSION AND NEWTON HOLMAN.

number people in Round Rock had organized their own Temperance Council. New Masonic lodges were founded in Bagdad (1871), Florence (1871), Macedonia (1874), and Liberty Hill (1875). Round Rock's first newspaper, the *Round Rock Sentinel*, printed its first issue in 1870 and published sporadically there until 1872, when its owner, Nat Q. Henderson, moved the paper to Georgetown. Another paper, the *Williamson County Record*, was also founded in Georgetown that year. Like the *Watchman*, all of these papers closed down by the late 1870s. They were supplanted by the *Williamson County Sun*, which was established in 1877 and is still being published today.

Prominent citizens of the county had been working since the early 1860s to organize institutions of higher learning. By 1867 enough money had been collected in Round Rock to construct a three-story building, and the Greenwood Masonic Institute (also known as Round Rock Academy) began holding classes; in 1881, after the Cumberland Presbyterian Church began to operate the school, it became known as Round Rock College. In Georgetown, a public subscription helped to raise funds to reorganize the Georgetown Male and Female School into Georgetown College. By 1871 a two-story rock building had been constructed, but when fund-raising lagged, the school's trustees offered it to the Methodist Church of Texas, which was already considering Georgetown as a possible site for a new college. The Methodists accepted, and by 1873 Texas University (later renamed Southwestern University) was offering classes to students from around the state.

Local citizens envisioned a great future for their county. Even as tens of thousands of longhorns were rumbling through the area, the editor of the *Watchman* presciently understood that the future development of Texas and Williamson County would come from another direction. "Ere many years," he wrote in 1870, "the whole length and breadth of our loved land will be checked with railways...[and] the products of our section will then go in exchange for luxuries of other countries. Already, thousands of immigrants are seeking our soil...sufficient to populate the entire country."

The simple but elegant Granger train station in the 1890s or early 1900s.

COURTESY OF THE WILLIAMSON COUNTY HISTORICAL COMMISSION AND ROBERT ROZACKY.

RAILROADS, IMMIGRANTS & COTTON

THE TRANSFORMATION OF WILLIAMSON COUNTY

As the *Watchman's* editor had predicted, many thousands of people moved into Williamson County between 1870 and 1900: its population rose from 6,368 in 1870 to 8,155 by 1880, to 25,909 by 1890, and to 38,072 by 1900. During the late nineteenth century, Williamson quickly became one of the most important cotton-producing areas in the state, and new cities, towns and communities emerged to serve its growing, more heterogenous population.

Some of the best farmland in the state lay in the blackland prairie of central Texas, including the eastern sections of Williamson County, but for many years its potential had remained for the most part untapped. As late as 1870, only 583 miles of railroad track had been laid in Texas. Without navigable rivers, Williamson was essentially landlocked, and the costs of transporting crops and other goods by wagon inhibited commercial farming there.

All that changed after 1876, when the International-Great Northern Railroad (also known as the I&GN), building west from Rockdale, extended its tracks into the county and opened it to development. Other railways would soon follow. After Georgetown was bypassed by the I&GN, a group of local investors formed the Georgetown Railroad Company. By December 1878, when the Georgetown Tap line was completed, a person could ride to Round Rock for fifty cents or to Austin for $1.30. In 1882 the Missouri, Kansas and Texas Railroad (known as the M-K-T, or Katy line) reached into Williamson County. The Katy was the first railroad to link Texas with the North, and it connected Williamson to the national economy as it had never been before. That same year the Austin and Northwestern, building a narrow-gauge line to link the capital to Abilene, extended its tracks through the southwestern corner of the county. In 1887, the Bastrop and Taylor Railway began to lay steel for another road connecting the county to South Texas.

Above: "C. Brady's Last Train as Conductor" on the Austin and Northwestern Railroad at Liberty Hill, 1890.

COURTESY OF THE WILLIAMSON COUNTY HISTORICAL COMMISSION AND MUSEUM.

Below: An early bird's-eye view of Taylor taken from the town's water tower looking west in 1878.

COURTESY OF THE TAYLOR PUBLIC LIBRARY.

In 1892 the Georgetown and Granger Railway Company began construction on a line between those two cities; after the initial investors experienced financial problems, the Missouri-Kansas-Texas (Katy line) bought the tracks, and, by 1904, had built a route that ran from Granger to Georgetown to Austin.

The rapid and cheap transportation offered by the railroads linked Williamson County with distant markets and population centers, encouraging immigration and the introduction of commercial farming into the area. As late as 1870 there were only 433 farms and ranches in the county, but the numbers rose rapidly after the railroads arrived: 1,538 farms by 1880; 2,841 by 1890; 4,403 by 1900. In 1870, only about 18,000 acres of farmland in the county had been classified as improved; by 1900, when farms had been established all across the eastern sections of blackland prairie, almost 300,000 acres were. And more than half of them were planted in cotton.

In 1869 the *Watchman* had counseled local farmers to "make cotton," and apparently at least some local farmers were listening. "[O]ld gins are being repaired, and new ones put up in many places," the *Watchman* noted in 1870. "Williamson County will hereafter be classed as one of the principal cotton counties." At that time, though, the cattle industry dominated the county's economy and cotton production was still limited. Local farmers harvested almost 209,000 bushels of corn in 1870, but ginned only 913 bales of cotton.

As the railroads brought thousands of new farmers to the area during the late nineteenth century, however, cotton cultivation spread rapidly across the county. Tens of thousands of acres of blackland prairie were opened by plows for the first time to plant the fiber, and even marginal soils in the western part of the county were devoted to it. By 1900 cotton was being grown on almost 153,000 acres in Williamson County; over 89,000 bales were ginned in Williamson in 1899-1900, more than in any other county in Texas. Cotton had become by far the county's most important crop, and easily the single most important element in the area's economy. Cotton cultivation was a way to make

money, but it was also much more than that: it came to shape the outlook, the culture, and the social rhythms of the area in profound ways.

The arrival of the railroads, the rapid proliferation of farming, and the invention of barbed wire put an end to the great cattle drives. A description of the county written in 1882 reported that the area was being "so rapidly enclosed in farms that there is scarcely sufficient open range left for large herds of cattle or horses." In Williamson, as in other parts of Texas, the introduction of barbed wire led to frictions between the new farmers who wanted to protect their crops, and the cattlemen who found that the fences increasingly blocked their access to water for their herds. In 1883, there were a number of fence-cutting incidents in the county.

By 1885, when the Snyders conducted their last cattle drive, it was clear that stockmen would have to adapt to the new conditions. Though cattle and sheep raising remained an important part of the local economy, ranchers fenced their herds, watered them with windmill-powered wells, and increasingly focused on improving the quality of their stock. Rather than driving their cattle hundreds of miles to distant markets, they took them to stockpens built at nearby railroad heads for transport by train.

The railroads, cotton, and immigration also led to a proliferation of new cities, towns, and communities. Taylor was the first city to grow out of the prairie. In May 1876, about a month before the International-Great Northern came through, the Texas Land Company (acting for the I&GN) bought 501 acres originally patented to George Glasscock, and now in the path of the rails. The company then divided the land into lots and called the new townsite "Taylorsville," after Edward Moses Taylor, a railroad official. The lots were auctioned off, creating an excitement in Williamson and surrounding counties. As a Rockdale newspaper noted, "The place is so situated as to command…the whole of the Belton and Bell County trade. Besides being in the center of one of the richest…sections of Texas, it is directly upon the great cattle trail." "Everything is stirring here," the paper continued. "People are rushing in, and the new town…is all the talk."

Taylorsville grew quickly. By 1879 only three years after it had been laid out, it boasted a bustling business district and a population of about 1,000. Though that year a devastating fire destroyed almost all of the original wooden buildings, these were replaced "almost overnight" by new, more substantial structures constructed mostly from brick brought in by rail. In 1882 the

Above: A view of Main Street in Hutto, 1890.

COURTESY OF THE WILLIAMSON COUNTY HISTORICAL COMMISSION AND CLARICE HANSTROM.

Below: An early bird's-eye view of Granger.

COURTESY OF THE WILLIAMSON COUNTY HISTORICAL COMMISSION AND ELIAS BIGON.

Henry Doering's general store in Walburg. Doering set up his store in 1882, and, in 1886, named the town that grew around it after his birthplace in Germany.

COURTESY OF THE WILLIAMSON COUNTY HISTORICAL COMMISSION AND LEONA KOKEL.

city was formally incorporated as Taylor (the old name must have sounded too undignified). That same year, when the Katy line built into the county, it intersected with the I&GN at Taylor, making the city one of the most important shipping centers for cotton, wool, and cattle in central Texas. By 1889 the city's population had grown to 2,547. By 1900 there were 4,211 people living in Taylor, which had already eclipsed Georgetown to become the county's largest city and its most important trade center.

Taylor was the largest new community to grow in the county after the railroads arrived, but many smaller ones followed. As the I&GN built through the county in 1876, its tracks traveled through ranchland owned by James Emory Hutto. After the rancher sold the railroad five acres for a townsite, a depot was built in 1877, and soon a new town, originally called Hutto Station, began to emerge. Thriving on the trade of surrounding cotton farmers, Hutto grew to a population of 563 by 1900, and within a few years its business section included a fine row of brick structures. When the I&GN bypassed the old town of Round Rock, the town, or much of it, moved to meet the tracks, and "New Round Rock" was born. A year later the new town included a number of businesses, including a bank, a hotel, a lumber yard, a livery stable, and a newspaper, the *Round Rock Headlight*. By 1890, over 1,400 people lived there.

Another community grew around the holdings of John R. Hoxie, a former mayor of Chicago and president of the I&GN. In 1878 Hoxie bought about 9,000 acres of ranchland east of Taylor and established a model ranch on his property, building stables, corrals, and a magnificent house renowned for the lavish parties held there for Hoxie's neighbors and eastern guests. Eventually a small town called Hoxie grew on the ranch; the village grew to include a school, a blacksmith shop, a general store and a cotton gin. In 1876 another community began to grow east of Taylor around an I&GN stop called Stiles Switch; it remained a tiny village until the early twentieth century, when it grew and was renamed Thrall.

New towns and cities also grew along the Katy line when it built into the county in the 1880s. In 1881, when it became known that the railroad would be coming through, John T. Bartlett and J. E. Peitzsch donated land near the Bell County line for a townsite. The new town, Bartlett, had a post office by October 1882, and a newspaper, the *Bartlett Headlight*, in 1886. By the time Bartlett incorporated in 1890, it already included a bank and a waterworks; by 1900, it had a population of almost a thousand people. By 1884 another town, eventually called Granger when it incorporated in 1891, had been established on the Katy a few miles south of Bartlett. Like Taylor, Hutto, Bartlett, and virtually every town in the county, Granger thrived on the cotton trade, and by 1899, according to one source, it had one of the three largest "ginneries" in the United States. About 940 people lived in Granger by 1900, when the town included a bank and a number of businesses including a newspaper, the *Granger News*. Another Katy depot was established at Circleville, where a small community had existed since the 1850s.

At about the same time as Hutto, Granger, and Bartlett were being established on the blackland prairie, the Austin and Northwestern line rearranged living patterns in the southwestern section of the county as it laid its narrow-gauge rails through the area. New villages like Rattan and Rutledge grew at flagstops along the line, while old communities like Pond Springs, Bagdad and Liberty Hill were bypassed. When the rails went through the village of Running Brushy, its name was changed—at the railroads request—to Brueggerhof, possibly the name of one of the line's owners. (In 1887, its name was changed again to Cedar Park.)

The transition was most traumatic for Bagdad. Since its founding in 1854, by 1880 the community had grown into a respectable town with a post office, several businesses, and even telephone service. Rather than run its tracks through the town, the railroad bypassed it and in 1882 laid out a new townsite called Leander (after Leander "Catfish" Brown, an official for the railroad) about a mile to the northeast. The old town of Bagdad slowly dried up as many of its citizens bought Leander townlots from the railroad and moved to the new site.

As noted earlier, Georgetown citizens had enabled their town to escape Bagdad's fate by building their own Tap line into Round Rock. Though it could not compete with Taylor as a major shipping center, the Tap enabled the city to survive as the county's seat of government and to gain a measure of prosperity itself by serving farmers and ranchers in the vicinity. A new county courthouse was built in 1877, and as new businesses were established the city grew steadily from a population of about 1,500 in 1878 to 2,970 by 1900.

While towns and cities were growing along Williamson County's new railway lines, scores of smaller farming communities were being created all across the county as the newcomers established schools and churches and sometimes cotton gins, stores and other businesses to service their localities.

In 1873, before the I&GN had built into the area, there had been thirty-one public schools in the county; by 1904 there were 105 school districts scattered across the county, each with at least one school. Most of these were small rural schools, one- or two-room frame buildings in which children of different ages and grade levels would study together under one or two teachers. But they, and the churches which were often built nearby, also served as the centers of community life and identity for the people who built them. The schools and churches, in other

A group photo taken at the Silent Grove School in Liberty Hill in the 1890s.

COURTESY OF THE WILLIAMSON COUNTY HISTORICAL COMMISSION AND LOGAN BRYSON.

❖

Above: A Czech farm family poses in front of their barn in the early 1900s near Granger.

COURTESY OF THE WILLIAMSON COUNTY HISTORICAL COMMISSION AND ELIAS BIGON.

Below: The interior of the Czech S. S. Cyril and Methodius Church in Granger in 1917.

COURTESY OF THE WILLIAMSON COUNTY HISTORICAL COMMISSION AND ELIAS PRIKRYRL.

words, often were the nuclei of the scores of rural communities established in the county during this period.

There were far too many to mention them all, but here's a sample: in the eastern part of the county emerged the communities of Beaukiss, Clark, Friendship, Guentzel, Laneport, Hare, New Bern, Noack, Polanka, Sandoval, Tidwell, Townsville, Turkey Creek, and Tyler. In the central sections grew Jackson, Neusser, Philadelphia, Robertson, Theon, Walburg, and Weir. In the western sections: Buttercup, Buttermilk, Cedar Grove, Chalk Ridge, Fisher, Gravel Hill, Concord, New Hope, Plough Handle, Prairie Lea, Primrose (also known as "Lick Skillet"), Rock House, and Seymour.

While many of those moving into Williamson County during the late nineteenth century were, like most of the first settlers, born in Texas or other southern states, the ethnic mix of the county changed during this period as thousands of European immigrants entered the area. In 1870, only 111 people in the county had foreign origins. By 1900 the Census counted 3,533 foreign-born people in Williamson, and they accounted for about nine percent of the county's total population.

Swedes, the first Europeans to migrate to the county in significant numbers, first begun to move into the area in 1853, when a Swedish widow, Mrs. Anna Palm, settled with her six sons on a farm just east of Round Rock. A log church was built there in 1861, and a small Swedish community called Palm Valley began to grow. During the 1870s and 1880s, Palm Valley became a focus for the county's increasing number of Swedes, who established farms and churches in the surrounding area and in communities like Round Rock, Weir, Hutto, Taylor, Jonah, and Georgetown. Swedes moved to the Williamson area partly because they knew they could find friendly assistance from fellow countrymen. The Palm family encouraged other Swedes to move into the area, sometimes providing work or financial assistance for those with little money. Carl Wegstrom, for example, who arrived in Round

Rock in June 1883, worked for the Palms for a year to pay for his passage to America. Through thrift and hard work Wegstrom eventually became a successful and well-respected farmer. In the late twentieth century, people of Swedish descent still told stories about John Anderson, who came to Williamson County in 1883 and set up a blacksmith shop in Georgetown. For many years immigrant Swedes had only to ask for "Blacksmith John" at the train station: they'd be taken to Anderson, who gave them food and shelter until they could find work. Carl "Cap" Hansen, a Danish immigrant, played a similar role in Hutto.

In the 1880s and 1890s the county also became home for many immigrants from central Europe. Beginning in the late 1880s, a number of Swiss immigrants settled on farms in the area north of Thrall. In 1893, after they built St. Paul's Lutheran Church and established a school, the village of New Bern began to emerge. Czechoslovakians and Moravians, who tended to cluster in or near Taylor, Granger, and Corn Hill, established Catholic and Czech Moravian churches in their communities; the beautiful Holy Trinity Catholic Church, which today towers over the Corn Hill area, is an example of their influence. Many German, Austrian, and Wendish immigrants also entered Williamson during the late nineteenth century, shaping the culture and development of communities such as Bartlett, Beyersville, Coupland, Macedonia, Noack, Neusser, Theon, Thrall, Walburg, and Waterloo.

Immigrant families often worked to preserve elements of their traditional heritage through their churches, schools, music, community events and family practices; a German-language

Above: The Dan Moody residence in Taylor was built in 1887.

COURTESY OF THE TAYLOR PUBLIC LIBRARY.

Below: John Darby in 1899, when many boys from prosperous families were dressed in this way.

COURTESY OF THE WILLIAMSON COUNTY HISTORICAL COMMISSION AND FAYE DUNCAN.

Above: An early photo of the Masonic Lodge building on Georgetown's courthouse square.

COURTESY OF THE GEORGETOWN HERITAGE SOCIETY.

Below: The delivery wagon for Ed Hunke's Bakery plies the streets of Taylor in the 1890s.

COURTESY OF THE TAYLOR PUBLIC LIBRARY.

weekly newspaper was being published in the county as early as 1889. Church services and, often, school sessions were conducted in many immigrant communities in the languages of the old country well into the twentieth century. In the early 1900s, for example, Swedes in the Union Hill area south of Georgetown organized classes to teach their children Swedish so they would not forget the mother tongue; in Granger, the Reverends Josef Barton and Joseph Hegar organized the Hus Memorial School for Czech children in the area.

Cultural differences, language barriers, and religious differences caused some native Texans to resent the immigrants. An early resident of the Coupland area decided to leave because, as he put it, "the Swedes and Johnson grass have come to this part of Texas and I don't want to be

Sam Loving of Round Rock, who enlisted in Company E, First Texas Volunteer Infantry during the Spanish-American War, shows his martial spirit in 1898. The First Texas eventually went to Cuba, but not until the war was over.

COURTESY OF THE WILLIAMSON COUNTY HISTORICAL COMMISSION AND CHARLIE LOVING.

around either one." The distance between the immigrant and native cultures was sometimes even reflected spacially; in Granger, for example, the Czechs and Germans tended to live on one side of the railroad tracks, the "Americans" on the other. Suspicions and resentments would become particularly intense during World War I, when the United States was at war with Germany and Austria-Hungary. Nevertheless, the new residents were generally accepted, and over the years they and their descendants have significantly shaped the economy and the culture of Williamson County.

African Americans also followed the cotton boom into Williamson during this period. While the Census counted 801 blacks in the county in 1870, their numbers rose steadily over the next thirty years: 1,631 by 1880; 2,755 by 1890; and 4,332 by 1900, when blacks made up about eleven percent of the county's total population. Hundreds of blacks moved to Georgetown and the new cities being built along the railroads; by the late 1880s, about twenty-five percent of Taylor's population was of African-American descent. Most blacks in the county, though, lived in the countryside. Some worked for small wages herding and tending livestock for local ranchers; many others grew cotton, probably most often as sharecroppers or farm laborers.

Since very little has been written about the lives of blacks in Williamson during the late nineteenth century, it is difficult to say exactly how or when African-Americans in the county were stripped of their full rights as citizens. Separate, "negro" schools were already established in the area by the 1870s and were probably in place earlier. But at least some blacks in the county may have been able to vote until the early 1900s. Given the patterns in nearby counties, it may be significant that the Republican presidential candidate (overwhelmingly favored by blacks at the time) received 2,151 votes in Williamson during the presidential election of 1896, and 1,812 votes in 1900, but only 614 in 1904 and only 245 by 1912.

Segregation may not have been as rigorously enforced during this period as is commonly assumed; Georgetown, for example, did not

The original St. John's Methodist Church and cemetery just south of Georgetown in 1900. The congregation moved to 311 East University Avenue in 1906.

COURTESY OF THE WILLIAMSON COUNTY HISTORICAL COMMISSION AND RUTH CARLSON.

make it illegal for blacks and whites to live in the same neighborhoods until the 1930s, and even then the law stated that "present residence" was "excepted" from its provisions. In any case, it is abundantly clear that during the late nineteenth century, and for many years to come, blacks in Williamson and elsewhere across Texas and the South had to live as second-class citizens, and were increasingly legally denied civic and social liberties accorded to others.

Many of the impressive Victorian homes and office buildings that graced the county's cities by the early twentieth century still stand today as testimony to the prosperity that the cotton trade could generate; quite a few of the county's citizens also profited by the sharp rise in property values that came with the railroads and the new cotton economy. It should also be pointed out, though, that as the nineteenth century came to a close, many of those, white and black, who actually planted and picked the cotton often received little in return for their efforts.

As late as 1880, before the largest waves of immigration into the area, almost eighty percent of Williamson's farmers tilled their own land; but by 1890, only forty-three percent of the county's farmers did, and, by 1900, fully six out of every ten farmers in the area were tenant farmers or sharecroppers who, whether they worked "on the halves," or "on the thirds and fourths" very likely had little if any money left from the cotton they grew after paying the debts they incurred to get out their crops. And, especially during the depression years of the 1890s when cotton prices plummeted, even farmers who owned their own land experienced difficult times. During the 1880s and 1890s the Grange and the Farmers Alliance, organizations that addressed the farmers' political and economic grievances, played an important role in local politics.

By 1900, Williamson County was a very different place than it had been only fifty years before, and oldtimers who had helped to settle the county must have marveled at the changes that had taken place within their own lifetimes. The Tonkawa and Comanches had long since been expelled. The land had been tamed and tilled; new cities had been built where once only grass grew; newly-built bridges spanned the San Gabriel and the Brushy. What had been an isolated wilderness was now tied to the rest of the nation by rail, by telegraph and telephone wire. But civilization carried a price. Gone were the buffalo, the wild steers and horses, and even most of the deer that had once roamed the area's prairies and brushlands; gone were the alligators from the streams. As late as 1885, a resident of the Matsler community had described what happened when an intense cold front blew in from the north across the prairie: "Suddenly, without warning the blue smoke rolled over the land.... Moisture in the peat suddenly met the cold wind, resulting in what was a blue steam-like vapor boiling up from the ground." After the prairie was plowed up for cotton and the peat was destroyed, "blue northers" were still cold, but they were no longer actually blue.

Girls and young women circle maypoles in a graceful Mayday celebration in Georgetown in the early 1900s.

COURTESY OF THE GEORGETOWN HERITAGE SOCIETY.

ROADSTERS, RADIOS & STILL MORE COTTON

WILLIAMSON COUNTY ENTERS THE TWENTIETH CENTURY

Many of the trends that had shaped Williamson County during the late 1800s continued into the early twentieth century. Railroad mileage grew, the population rose, and cotton increasingly dominated the local economy. Most people in the county still lived in the many small, isolated communities that had mushroomed in the area over the past fifty years, their everyday lives tuned to the rhythms of the agricultural cycle. But as always, change was as constant as continuity. The ethnic mix of the county shifted significantly again between 1900 and 1930. Meanwhile life in cities like Georgetown and Taylor became more comfortable and sophisticated, and by the 1920s the rapid adoption of new technology in the form of automobiles, tractors, and radios opened new possibilities for people in the county and began to break down old ways of life.

As Williamson County residents looked ahead to the new century, the changes that already had occurred encouraged them to cherish and preserve the past. In 1899, Confederate veterans in the county began to hold reunions in various locations, and out of these grew the Old Settlers Association, which held its first meeting in 1904. Its charter specifically limited membership to white citizens of the county. Perhaps in response to this restriction, but in keeping with the basic motives of those who had formed the Old Settlers, blacks in the county formed their own group. In 1908, the black leader Frank Hasty worked to form the Ex-Slave Union Association of Industry, which held an organizational barbeque in Taylor on October 24 and 25 that year.

The annual reunions of the Old Settlers Association were for many years among the county's greatest social events, combining good times with constant reminders of what life had been like for the area's first settlers. On August 23, 24, and 25, 1906, for example, thousands of people attended the Association's third annual reunion. Many families arrived on Thursday and camped in Glasscock Springs Park (now San Gabriel Park), "entertaining themselves by singing hymns and folk songs." Over the next two days, the growing crowds were treated to a number of speeches and lots of music, including an "old fiddler's contest." Meanwhile, scattered around the grounds were exhibits of historical "relics" that brought to life the area's pioneer heritage—old guns, gristmills, weaving looms, and a six-yoke ox team.

Construction of the last railroad to build across Williamson County began after 1909, when a group of outside investors chartered the Bartlett-Florence Railway company and began to lay tracks in the northern part of the county. As in the past, new towns and communities appeared as the rail progressed westward. In 1909 the little village of Schwertner began to grow larger when Adolf Schwertner, a German immigrant who had settled in the area in 1877, donated a townsite on the tracks; before long, the town included two cotton gins, a bank, at least two blacksmiths, a school, a saloon, and a lumberyard.

In December that same year, town lots were sold for another new town, Jarrell, that was in the projected path of the rails. By the time the road finally was completed to Florence, small communities had begun to appear at a number of other stops along the way. Since four of these were given Biblical names (St. Matthew, St. Mark, St. Luke, St. John), the railroad came to be called "the Four Gospels Line." The old town of Corn Hill, established in the 1850s, began to die after many of its residents, bypassed by the railroad, began to move to Jarrell. In 1915 S. A. Keeling used a steam-powered tractor to haul at least twenty houses from Corn Hill to the new site.

Meanwhile, on the blackland prairie large old ranches were being cut up and sold to farmers as cotton cultivation continued to spread. In 1908 the heirs of John Sparks (once one of the county's most prominent cattlemen, and later the governor of Nevada) divided his old ranch south of Taylor. The Hoxie Ranch, established back in the 1880s, was subdivided in 1910, its famous mansion left mostly unoccupied until 1934, when it burned down. By 1910 almost 220,000 acres in the county were planted in cotton, and the trend continued: by 1930 more than 268,000 acres in Williamson were devoted to cotton, fully seventy-two percent of the cropland harvested in the county that year.

As cotton farming expanded between 1900 and 1930, the county's population continued to

Above: Joe Spivey in chaps, after fording a river in 1916. He later became a county constable.

COURTESY OF THE WILLIAMSON COUNTY HISTORICAL COMMISSION AND GARY SPIVEY.

Below: Irene and John Darby's wedding photo taken in Florence, October 1910. She was sixteen and he was eighteen.

COURTESY OF THE WILLIAMSON COUNTY HISTORICAL COMMISSION AND FAYE DUNCAN.

Above: A postcard picture of the International & Great Northern Railroad's shops in Taylor during the early 1900s.

COURTESY OF GEORGE MEYER.

Below: Frances Cmerek feeding chickens near Granger in the 1910s.

COURTESY OF THE WILLIAMSON COUNTY HISTORICAL COMMISSION AND NANCIE PAVLISKA RODDY.

rise, though more slowly than before: by 1930 there were 44,146 people living in the area. Most of the increase occurred because of continuing immigration. About a thousand people born in foreign countries other than Mexico migrated to the county between 1900 and the end of 1914, when the First World War virtually closed off immigration from abroad. Though the number of native whites in the population actually declined somewhat during this period, Williamson County's black population grew rapidly, rising more than sixty-one percent between 1900 and 1930; that year, the census counted 7,056 blacks in the county, almost sixteen percent of the total population. Meanwhile, thousands of Mexican nationals began moving to the area.

Tejanos had been living in Williamson since the earliest days of the county, and during the late 1800s and early 1900s, a slow trickle of immigrants from Mexico helped to maintain a the small Latino presence in the area; in 1910 there were 294 people in the county who had been born in Mexico. Between 1910 and 1930, however, the political and economic miseries associated with the Mexican Revolution encouraged hundreds of thousands of Mexicans to move north to Texas. In 1930, the Census counted 4,967 people of Mexican descent in Williamson.

❖

Above: Before refrigerators, ice wagons rolled through the streets of Georgetown and other communities in the county.

COURTESY OF THE GEORGETOWN HERITAGE SOCIETY.

Bottom, left: Loraine Castro Camacho (left) and Frank Camacho, Mexican-American children on a tenant farm near Thrall in the 1920s.

COURTESY OF THE WILLIAMSON COUNTY HISTORICAL COMMISSION AND DANIEL C. CAMACHO.

Bottom, right: Lorraine Castro Camacho, seen in the picture on the left, ten years later when she was the queen of a Diez y Sies celebration in the 1930s.

COURTESY OF THE WILLIAMSON COUNTY HISTORICAL COMMISSION AND DANIEL C. CAMACHO.

The result was another significant shift in the county's ethnic mix. In 1900, even after many blacks and European immigrants had moved into the area, native-born whites still constituted almost eighty percent of its population. By 1930, though, only sixty-seven percent (about two out of three) were native-born whites, and many of these were the children and grandchildren of the thousands of European immigrants who had moved to the area over the previous fifty years. Partly because of the continuing cotton boom, Williamson County's population had become an even more diverse mix of people from many different backgrounds and cultures.

❖

Left: Tom Young (with bow tie, center) on his way to the gallows on March 30, 1906. "Trust in Jesus Christ and he will save you," he said just before he was hanged. "I'm happier now than ever before in my life."

COURTESY OF THE GEORGETOWN HERITAGE SOCIETY.

Bottom: Thousands of people gathered to watch the hanging of murderer Tom Young in March 1906. It was the last public hanging in Williamson County.

COURTESY OF THE GEORGETOWN HERITAGE SOCIETY.

Most of the county's Mexican immigrants worked as agricultural laborers or sharecroppers, but by the 1920s hundreds of them had settled in Round Rock, Taylor, and Georgetown. Separate "Mexican" facilities were established. The Mexican Mission Chapel, operated in Georgetown by D.W. Carter, doubled as a school—"for lack of a school building"—by 1923. In Taylor, Mexican and Mexican-American students took their lessons at the Alamo School; Round Rock rented a church for the purpose until 1934, when, with financial aid from the Texas Relief Commission, the Round Rock Independent School District built a new

Above: A thresher steam tractor on the Mathias farm, one mile outside Walburg, in 1913.

COURTESY OF THE WILLIAMSON COUNTY HISTORICAL COMMISSION AND LEONA KOKEL.

Below: The west side of Main Street in Granger in 1916.

COURTESY OF THE WILLIAMSON COUNTY HISTORICAL COMMISSION AND THE ROSENBERG FAMILY.

schoolhouse for its Latino children. Lessons ended at the third grade.

During the generally prosperous years of the early twentieth century most of the county's cities continued to grow as new businesses and industries were spun off the cotton economy and the money it brought to people in the area. Proclaiming itself "The World's Greatest Inland Cotton Market," Taylor remained the most important trade center for the surrounding countryside. In the early 1900s the streets in the city's thriving business district were paved, and its gins, compresses, railroad yards, banks, stores, and other businesses attracted farmers from all around the surrounding area; entertainment—from plays to music to wrestling matches—could be found at the opera house. Every July from 1881 until 1916, the city also hosted an annual fair, which featured a parade, music, horse races, and a number of contests.

Thanks to its location on the railroads, Taylor attracted more industrial development than the other cities in the county. The Taylor Bedding Manufacturing Company, organized in 1906, grew to become by 1930 "one of the largest mattress factories in the South." At peak production, its 400 employees could produce 2,500 mattresses, or fill five railroad cars full of upholstering felt, in a single day. By that time Taylor also had two oil refineries, which fed on petroleum pumped out of the ground by oil wells a few miles southeast of the city. As Taylor grew steadily during the early twentieth century, its population rose to 5,965 by 1920 and to 7,463 by 1930, when, according to one source, seventy-five percent of the people living there were whites, fifteen percent were blacks, and about ten percent were Mexican immigrants.

Though overshadowed by Taylor, Georgetown's role as the county seat of government remained secure as the city slowly grew and prospered. A new county courthouse, designed by C. H. Page of Austin, was completed in 1911; the building, renovated (with some changes to the exterior) in 1965, is still in use today. As the trading center for nearby farmers, Georgetown also developed some

Left: Candy Jim's candy store and theater (in background) at 303 North Main Street in Taylor, 1910.

COURTESY OF THE TAYLOR PUBLIC LIBRARY.

Bottom, left: A gusher at the Thrall oil fields.

COURTESY OF THE JOHNSON-ELLYSON ESTATE.

Bottom, right: Taylor's Buckhorn Saloon, with owner Hank Sakewitz.

COURTESY OF THE WILLIAMSON COUNTY HISTORICAL COMMISSION AND LINDA BOATRIGHT.

small industrial concerns, such as the impressive cottonseed-oil plant that still stands near Sixteenth Street west of Austin Avenue.

The most dramatic economic event in the county during the early twentieth century undoubtedly occurred in 1915, when oil was discovered on the Fritz Fuchs place, about a mile south of Thrall. News of the strike brought hundreds of drillers, fieldworkers, and campfollowers flooding into the area. Thrall became a boomtown, and its population quickly jumped to over 3,000. Though over a hundred wells were drilled in the area, the boom was over within a few years, and by 1920 only 272 people remained in Thrall. Another brief oil boom began in 1930 after a strike on J. C. Abbott's land near Lawrence Chapel, but it died out when the field proved to be too shallow for sustained production.

Though industries were beginning to become more important to the local economy, cotton remained at the center of the county's life and identity. A visitor to Taylor in the late fall in the early 1900s, at cotton-picking time, could sense the excitement in the air; this was the time when everyone made some money and could look forward to spending at least a little. On Sunday afternoons, area farmers drove their wagons into the city, picking up blacks they hired to help with the harvest; often, the city's domestic workers would get a week off to pick. All week, lines of wagons, loaded high to their sideboards with fleecy white cotton, waited for their turn at the city's many gins; the cottonyards were piled with great stacks of bales ready to be compressed and shipped.

Cotton picking was grueling work. Hauling large canvas sacks behind them, the pickers crawled or hunched their way down the rows, rapidly snatching the cotton from the bolls, tossing it into the sacks, crawling and snatching again and again. Full sacks were weighed, the picker was credited, the cotton poured into a wagon; then back to the rows, crawling and picking again. A first-rate cotton picker in a good patch could harvest more than 1,000 pounds of cotton in a day, but anyone who could pull 500 pounds in a day was thought to be good. J. H. Boswell, who lived in Taylor during this time, later remembered that while picking cotton was "hard work," it was also "a welcome change from ordinary duties as well as quite a social occasion, with much talking and visiting." Pickers from town took mattresses and food with them to the fields, and slept where they picked until the next Saturday, when they were taken back to town and paid for their work: about fifty cents for every hundred pounds picked.

As late as 1920, the combined population of Williamson County's six largest cities and towns—Taylor, Georgetown, Granger, Bartlett, Round Rock, and Florence—accounted for only 14,061 people, or about one-third of the county's total population. While these urban areas continued to grow as the region moved further into the twentieth century, most people living in the county still lived on farmsteads or in the small communities spread out across the region. It is difficult for us

Opposite, from top to bottom: The Monodale cotton gin in Hutto.
COURTESY OF THE WILLIAMSON COUNTY HISTORICAL COMMISSION AND GERRY ANDERSON.

Cornelius Bloom , Einar Stried, and Roland Stried on cotton bales near Round Rock.
COURTESY OF THE WILLIAMSON COUNTY HISTORICAL COMMISSION AND DANA NOREN.

Wagons loaded with cotton at the Fred Harrison gin in Jarrell, c. 1920s.
COURTESY OF THE WILLIAMSON COUNTY HISTORICAL COMMISSION AND MARY HODGE.

A truck hauling cotton bales south of Taylor in the 1920s.
COURTESY OF THE TAYLOR PUBLIC LIBRARY.

Top: The Taylor High School football team in 1915.
COURTESY OF THE TAYLOR PUBLIC LIBRARY.

Bottom: Vander Clyde Broadway, whose stage name was "Barbette," grew up in Round Rock. Inspired by a circus performance he saw in Austin as a child, he practiced walking a tight-wire on his mother's laundry line. By the 1920s, "Barbette" was one of the most acclaimed performance artists in Paris, France. Jean Cocteau called him "one of the most beautiful things in the theater."
COURTESY OF THE AUSTIN HISTORY CENTER, AUSTIN PUBLIC LIBRARY.

today to imagine just how isolated most of these people were from those who lived just ten, fifteen or twenty miles away. Though telephones and automobiles were beginning to spread around the county in the 1910s they were still far from universal, and radio sets were still unknown. Rural electrification was still several decades away.

A trip that would take minutes today required hours then. The roads that did exist were almost all unpaved and unreliable in bad weather, and even moderate rains could render unbridged creeks uncrossable for many hours. For most farm families, weeks passed between journeys to Georgetown, Taylor, Bartlett, or Granger, and an excursion to Austin by train to see the circus or a show was a rare and cherished event. In 1998 Hugh Davenport, who was born on a farm near Hutto in 1908, still vividly recalled the day, more than eighty years ago, when he and his mother took the train from Round Rock to Austin to see a performance of *Peter Pan*.

Not "privileged" yet to enjoy the benefits of television, radio, VCRs and internet access, people naturally looked elsewhere for entertainment, instruction, and meaning. Though practices varied according to the traditions followed by the county's various ethnic groups, most people relied on their families and their neighbors for entertainment. Music and singing helped pass many hours: women commonly learned to play the piano, and most families that could afford a piano found a way to get one. Families—and sometimes, entire communities—gathered to sing old, well-known hymns and traditional tunes.

Family traditions were passed on from father to son, mother to daughter. On summer evenings, after work was done, as families sat on their front porches (before air conditioning, that was the only cool place to sit), parents and grandparents passed old family stories on to the children.

Top, left: Pet Brown (1888-1923) from Taylor, World Middleweight Wrestling Champion in 1914.

COURTESY OF THE TAYLOR PUBLIC LIBRARY.

Top, right: The Pet Brown Wrestling Club in Taylor, 1920.

COURTESY OF THE WILLIAMSON COUNTY HISTORICAL COMMISSION AND FRED AND JUANITA ROOSE.

Below: The town of Schwertner, seen in the distance with smoke stack, c. 1900. Note the condition of the road in the foreground.

COURTESY OF THE WILLIAMSON COUNTY HISTORICAL COMMISSION AND STANLEY SCHWERTNER.

And the children, in spite of themselves, perhaps, listened and remembered. Story-telling was something of an art form, and a good story-teller could hold an audience for hours. On Sundays after church services, families would pile into a wagon—or later, into an auto—and visit with relatives in the area, spending the rest of the day and much of the evening talking, listening. We shouldn't go too far to romanticize this way of life—family tensions, animosities, and even feuds were not unknown—but people alive at the time remember, almost sadly now, the intimate, interconnected feel of the society they once knew.

Religion—whether Baptist, Methodist, A.M.E., or Catholic—played a significant role in the lives of most families and communities; in fact, in many small communities, the local church was the single most important social institution. In the Lawler community in the northwestern part of the county, the Lawler Baptist Church brought people together for worship, Sunday "singings," community suppers, picnics and other events. Women in the community sometimes held quilting parties; young folks would have "play parties," which included parlor games, "candy breaking" and a lot of cakes. "It was not uncommon to have a dozen layer cakes," Effie McCleod remembered many years later. "It was truly fun."

In formal and informal ways local churches shaped the behavior of the people in their communities. The Lawler Baptists, for example,

❖

Above: Traveling preachers of the Primitive Baptist faith on an oxcart in the early 1900s. The sign reads "Traveling Through Ark[ansas] Will Be Home Soon."

COURTESY OF THE WILLIAMSON COUNTY HISTORICAL COMMISSION AND RALPH DIXON LOVE.

Below: Part of the congregation of the Immanuel Lutheran Church in Taylor during the early 1900s. The man with the hat in his hand in the center of the photo is Karl Brandenburg, a German immigrant and a charter member of the church.

COURTESY OF THE WILLIAMSON COUNTY HISTORICAL COMMISSION AND LINDA BOATRIGHT.

could and sometimes did expel church members caught using foul language, attending horse races on Sunday, or doing anything else they considered "unchristian conduct." A number of communities in the county, including Georgetown, banned the sale of alcohol long before the Prohibition amendment was adopted by Congress in 1917.

During summer months, the county's many Baptist churches often hosted camp revival meetings. Dozens, sometimes hundreds of people from many miles around would gather for a week or more to visit with family and friends, and to recharge their spiritual lives. Romances sparked and developed; old ties were

Top, left: Picking cotton on the Pavliska farm west of Granger in the early 1900s. The babe-in-arms to the left is Nancy Pavliska, two-years-old, in a sunbonnet.

COURTESY OF THE WILLIAMSON COUNTY HISTORICAL COMMISSION AND NANCIE PAVLISKA RODDY.

Top, right: Picking cotton in a field near Round Rock in 1912 are Agda Noren (left) and Annie Friedholm.

COURTESY OF THE WILLIAMSON COUNTY HISTORICAL COMMISSION AND DANA NOREN.

Middle: Williamson County residents dressed in traditional costumes of the Allied nations during World War I. This photo was taken in Theon in 1918.

COURTESY OF THE WILLIAMSON COUNTY HISTORICAL COMMISSION AND THE JOHNSON-ELLYSON ESTATE.

Bottom: "The Hour of Victory." Granger residents celebrate the end of World War I on November 11, 1918. The sign to the left reads "To Hell with the Kaiser."

COURTESY OF THE WILLIAMSON COUNTY HISTORICAL COMMISSION AND DAN MARTINETS.

Top: Just home from church in Taylor are Otis Hatch and his wife, Lee Aldich Hatch, and their children, c. 1920s.

COURTESY OF THE WILLIAMSON COUNTY HISTORICAL COMMISSION AND LESLIE HILL.

Middle: First Communion Day for Mexican-American girls of Our Lady of Guadalupe Church in Taylor in the 1930s.

COURTESY OF THE WILLIAMSON COUNTY HISTORICAL COMMISSION AND DANIEL C. CAMACHO.

Bottom: Men loading cotton onto a truck near Hutto; the date of this photo is uncertain, but it could possibly have been taken in the 1930s.

COURTESY OF THE WILLIAMSON COUNTY HISTORICAL COMMISSION AND FLO THOMPSON.

Above: The Czech Moravian Brethren Church in Granger, 1915.

COURTESY OF THE WILLIAMSON COUNTY HISTORICAL COMMISSION AND DAN MARTINETS.

Below: Mourners at Reverend Frantisek Pridal's funeral in front of a church in Granger, 1927.

COURTESY OF THE WILLIAMSON COUNTY HISTORICAL COMMISSION AND EVELYN SLADECEK PEKAR.

remembered and renewed. Sometimes memorable moments grew out of practical jokes. According to one story, a renowned preacher imported for a revival in the county continually exhorted his audience to think about what would happen to them if the world came to an end. What would be the state of your soul, he asked again and again, if Gabriel's horn blew tomorrow? The next day he demanded the same, but more insistently: "What will you do? What will you do? I can hear Gabriel's horn a-blowin' now!" he shouted. "I can hear it now!" At that moment, a trumpet blast erupted from a nearby tree and the preacher, eyes wide, began

to run. A prankster had waited in that tree for hours with a borrowed horn to get a laugh.

In those days before families owned freezers and refrigerators, fresh meat was impossible to keep for long. Many communities organized beef clubs; members took turns supplying cattle, then divided the slaughtered beef amongst themselves for quick consumption. Hog killings could also be community affairs. When a farmer slaughtered one of his hogs, neighbors who helped were rewarded with a flour sack full of meat, and by being treated to a delicious picnic lunch that included heaping plates of roasted ribs and tenderloin served with brown gravy, biscuits, milk, and coffee.

For a number of reasons this traditional, community-oriented way of life, which was

Top, left: Members of the Osuna family, who were sharecroppers on the "Dunlop Place" near Andice, in an early stage of butchering a hog, 1949. After the hog's throat was cut, the carcass was dipped into scalding water to help remove the hair.

COURTESY OF THE WILLIAMSON COUNTY HISTORICAL COMMISSION AND THE OSUNA FAMILY.

Top, right: An early photo of the fifth (and, so far, the last) Williamson County Courthouse. Built in 1910-1911, it was remodeled in 1965.

COURTESY OF THE WILLIAMSON COUNTY HISTORICAL COMMISSION AND ANDREW ANDERSON.

Below: The Martinets Bros. country store near Granger, 1915.

COURTESY OF THE WILLIAMSON COUNTY HISTORICAL COMMISSION AND DAN MARTINETS.

Top, left: This crowded street scene in Thrall in 1915 shows some of the effects of the oil boom that briefly flourished there.

COURTESY OF THE WILLIAMSON COUNTY HISTORICAL COMMISSION AND JERRY FLEMING.

Top, right: Waymon and Artie Ferrell during their courting days, c. 1916.

PHOTO COURTESY OF IRENE VARAN.

Below: The Rock House schoolhouse, near Andice, in the late 1910s or '20s. By the late 1990s, nothing remained of the Rock House community but a few crumbling foundations.

COURTESY OF THE WILLIAMSON COUNTY HISTORICAL COMMISSION AND RALPH DIXON LOVE.

rooted in the cotton culture and rural isolation, began to be undermined during the 1910s and 1920s. Automobiles were considered an expensive luxury when the first few appeared in the county in the early 1900s. In 1909, there were only ninety-six autos in Williamson County, and all but twenty of them were owned by people who lived in Taylor, Georgetown, Bartlett, Hutto, and Round Rock. But less expensive models began to appear in the 1910s, and by the late 1920s almost anyone could own an auto of some sort. Almost 6,300 cars were registered in Williamson by 1922, and, by 1930, the number had grown to almost 12,000—more than one for every four people living in the county at the time.

Meanwhile, the state, county and city governments began to spend many hundreds of thousands of dollars to improve roads in the area. By the early 1920s, three state highways had been built through the county: the King's Highway, which ran from Taylor north through Circleville and Granger; the Meridian Highway, which followed the approximate route of present-day Interstate 35; and the Robert E. Lee

❖

Top, left: Nancy Earl, who worked as a cook for the Nelson family in Round Rock for many years, c. 1929. Note that she is smoking a cigar.

COURTESY OF THE WILLIAMSON COUNTY HISTORICAL COMMISSION AND THE NELSON ESTATE.

Top, right: Charles and Mattie Townsend in Granger, 1927.

COURTESY OF THE WILLIAMSON COUNTY HISTORICAL COMMISSION AND MILDRED TOWNSEND.

Below: "Ring Around the Rosie." Adults and children play a game dating back to the Middle Ages. The date and location where this photo was taken are uncertain; possibly Florence in the 1910s.

COURTESY OF THE WILLIAMSON COUNTY HISTORICAL COMMISSION AND FLO THOMPSON.

Highway, which ran northwest out of Austin through Liberty Hill. Other roads around the county were being graveled about this same time, including one following the approximate route of present-day State Highway 79.

Farmers' lives were also changed during this period by the introduction of tractors and other new equipment for mechanized farming. A man driving a tractor could cultivate many more acres than the same man behind a mule, and the work was less demanding. During the 1910s and 1920s, more and more local farmers began to acquire these labor-saving machines. A tractor dealer in Schwertner attracted good business by accepting farmers' work animals as partial payment; dozens of mules and horses received in trade were herded into a corral near where the Schwertner Bank is now located. A possibly apocryphal story holds that one old farmer who had never driven before lost his head completely while taking a test drive at the Schwertner dealership. Unable to get his new tractor to stop, he ended up driving around in tight circles pulling at the wheel, shouting "Whoa! Whoa!" Like autos, tractors soon began to change the dynamics of farming and living in the area.

Above: After record-setting rain, flood waters devastated many parts of the county in September 1921. This was the scene in Granger.

COURTESY OF THE WILLIAMSON COUNTY HISTORICAL COMMISSION AND DAN MARTINETS.

Below: This general store in Taylor even carried buggies for its customers.

COURTESY OF THE TAYLOR PUBLIC LIBRARY.

Automobiles and the expanding road network gave farming families in Williamson County mobility they could not have imagined just a few years earlier. By the late 1920s and early 1930s, cars and another mass-marketed invention—the radio receiver—were connecting them ever more closely with the outside world, breaking down the isolation in which they had lived. Farmers, of course, welcomed their new freedom, but most could not possibly foresee that their county's cotton economy—and their way of life, which it supported—would soon be shattered by the cumulative effects of mechanization, an economic catastrophe, and world-wide war.

Franciso Castro driving his mule-drawn trash wagon in downtown Taylor in 1949. He reluctantly switched to tractor power the next year.

COURTESY OF THE WILLIAMSON COUNTY HISTORICAL COMMISSION AND DANNY C. CAMACHO.

Depression, Drought & Mechanization

The Decline of the Cotton Culture

During the first twenty years of the twentieth century, farmers and merchants in the Williamson County area experienced a certain level of prosperity; high prices for cotton during the First World War (1914-1918) especially helped to buoy the area economy. During the 1920s, though, declining prices, droughts, growing problems with soil depletion and boll weevils, and the terrible flood of 1921 all combined to drag the local economy down. Though acreage devoted to cotton in the county increased by about eighteen percent between 1920 and 1930, the number of bales produced actually dropped more than twelve percent.

As prices dropped and yields declined, cotton farmers in the area were planting more and more cotton to try to make the same money they had enjoyed earlier; but other farmers all over the south were doing the same thing, and the world's supply of cotton far outstripped demand for it. In 1928, a pretty good year for farmers in the area, cotton sold for twenty-eight cents a pound. After the New York Stock Exchange crashed in October 1929, cotton plunged to sixteen cents and like the rest of the nation—like the rest of the world—the people of Williamson County faced the Great Depression. By 1931, cotton was selling for five cents a pound.

As almost all of the county's banks closed, people lost their savings and loans became about impossible to get; many local farmers lost their lands. As Adolf Wolbrueck later remembered, "it just kept getting worse and worse and worse." The destitute lived on the ground or in tents; the county courthouse was opened to those who had nowhere else to sleep. Many people took any work they could get, for whatever pay: "You got a dollar a day [then], you were in good money," Jessie Labit recalled. Hoboes and tramps with nowhere to go wandered through the county hoping for handouts; some trees in the Loafer's Glory community still bear the marks these people left to show which households would be friendly and which would not.

After 1933, when Franklin Roosevelt began his New Deal, county residents began to benefit from federal programs designed to relieve poverty and pump money into the economy. As the Depression seemed to grind on endlessly, the Works Progress Administration (WPA) hired local men and women for a number of different projects. In Round Rock, men working for the WPA dug through solid rock with picks and shovels to install sewer lines. In Georgetown, WPA workers made a number of improvements to San Gabriel Park, including the construction of the park building that is now used as a community center. In Hutto, the WPA paid men to clean up empty lots and to work on the streets.

The WPA extended and improved the county's growing network of roads and operated quarries in the county that supplied the rock used to construct a number of buildings at the University of Texas in Austin. People were also employed by the WPA to organize and catalogue county records, and to write brief histories of the county and some of its cities. Other New Deal programs helped to relieve the worst effects of the Depression, too. Some of the county's young men found temporary work with the Civilian Conservation Corps (CCC), while others were hired by the National Youth Administration (NYA) to build furniture for public buildings. Women worked in the WPA history project, in canning kitchens, and in sewing circles making clothes for the poor.

Another source of help for a number of farmers was the Round Rock Cheese Factory. Established in 1928, the factory already had a reputation for quality production by 1929, when it won a first prize at the Texas State Fair. During the Depression, its trucks crisscrossed the southern sections of the county picking up milk from local farmers. The factory was the chief source of income for many farmers during this period, and there are people in the area who remember those trucks fondly to this day.

Cotton production in the county fell dramatically during the Great Depression, as farmers were hammered by droughts, low prices, and the evaporation of credit. In 1930, at the onset of the Depression, over 268,000 acres were planted in cotton in Williamson, and more

❖

Right: The Jonah community, probably in the 1920s or 30s.

COURTESY OF THE WILLIAMSON COUNTY HISTORICAL COMMISSION AND HARLAN HAYES.

Below: Skins of possums, minks, and raccoons drying on Joe Cmerek, Sr.'s farm west of Granger. Cmerek's sons, Victor, Rudolph, and Alfonse trapped animals during the Great Depression and sold the pelts for twenty cents to a dollar each.

COURTESY OF THE WILLIAMSON COUNTY HISTORICAL COMMISSION AND HATTIE CMEREK.

Left: Despite their many disappointments and problems during the Great Depression, county residents still had the spirit to stage this parade in the 1930s.

COURTESY OF THE WILLIAMSON COUNTY HISTORICAL COMMISSION AND LEONA KOKEL.

Below: On excursion are (from left to right) Boyd Faught, Hazel Day, and James Hood at Lion's Head on the north fork of the San Gabriel River, Georgetown about 1936.

COURTESY OF THE WILLIAMSON COUNTY HISTORICAL COMMISSION AND JAMES AND HAZEL HOOD.

than 68,000 bales were produced; by 1940, only about 139,000 acres were devoted to cotton and production had plummeted to fewer than 37,000 bales. Hundreds of farmers were driven off the land: during those Depression years the number of farms in the county fell by almost twenty percent, and by 1940 only 3,945 were left. Hardest hit were tenant farmers and sharecroppers, whose already precarious existence was increasingly undermined by mechanization and new government policies.

In the New Deal's attempt to help farmers to raise the price of cotton and other crops by reducing the supply, the federal Agricultural Adjustment Administration provided cash payments to farmers who reduced their cotton acreage. In one sense, at least, the practice worked: in Texas the number of acres planted in cotton fell more than fifty percent between 1930 and 1939, while the government paid out about $50 million to the farmers involved. Though the letter of the law obliged landowners participating in the program to share a percentage of their payments with their tenants and sharecroppers, in practice the complicated, ambiguous formulas designed for the program encouraged the owners

HAS BOMBED TOKIO—Now on a two-weeks' urlough to visit his parents in Taylor is Lieut. Wilder, who received his decora on in ington recently as a result of having accompanied Gen. James Doolittle across the enemy's capital city. Shown are his mother, whose birthday coincides with her son's return, his father, L. A. Wilder, and his brother and sister, Mrs. N. G. Holman.

❖

Above: Ross Wilder, who flew in the famous Doolittle Raid that bombed Tokyo in 1942, is shown here on a furlough with his family in Taylor later that year.

COURTESY OF THE TAYLOR PUBLIC LIBRARY.

Below: Emzie Fisher with his infant son, Lester, during World War II.

COURTESY OF THE WILLIAMSON COUNTY HISTORICAL COMMISSION AND LESTER FISHER.

to let their tenants and croppers go. As Neil Foley writes in his book *White Scourge*, "Thus, one of the consequences of reducing the surplus of cotton through cotton payments was the creation of a surplus of sharecroppers and tenants." If less cotton was going to be grown, fewer people would be needed to do it; and as more and more tractors were employed, fewer and fewer farmers would be.

In 1930 almost seventy percent of the farmers in Williamson County had been tenant farmers and sharecroppers, but during the 1930s more than thirty percent of them either left the land or were reduced to becoming farm laborers. As a result, during the Depression Williamson County's population declined for the first time since the Civil War. In 1940, the Census counted 41,698 people living in the area, a five percent drop in one decade. As people moved out of the county, some of the smaller communities could no longer support their schools, and their districts were consolidated with others nearby: Nyman (school consolidated 1932), Long Branch (1932), Gattis (1939), and Caldwell Heights (1941) began to disappear.

Although Williamson County began to escape from the Depression after 1941, when the United States entered the Second World War, the war did not reverse other trends established during the 1930s. There were still about 8,000 mules in Williamson County in 1939, but soon they would all be replaced by tractors. Ranching and poultry were becoming more important to the area's economy now. And as the area's cotton production and population continued to decline, so would many of the small communities that the cotton boom had created.

In 1940, a traveler passing through Round Rock wrote that the town seemed "much like an old person sitting quietly beside the highway, ready to tell a story." Between 1941 and 1945, this "sleepy" little town contributed over 350 of its citizens to fight against Germany and Japan, and over the course of the war thousands of men and women in the county joined the armed services. Some of them witnessed historic events. Ross Wilder, from Taylor, participated in the famous Doolittle Raid in 1942, when American planes first bombed Tokyo; Joe Stiborik, also from Taylor, was aboard the *Enola Gay* when, on August 6, 1945, the plane dropped its atomic bomb on Hiroshima. Even those servicemen who never left the United

States were often introduced to new places, new ways of life, new skills, and opportunities that they would otherwise never have known.

At home, Williamson County's citizens helped to promote the war effort by participating in war bond drives, collecting scrap, and learning to get along with limited supplies of rationed items like sugar, tires, and gasoline. Children scanned the skies looking for Nazi planes. The war also created lucrative economic opportunities for men and women in the county who had been displaced from farms and other jobs during the Depression. During and just after the war many people moved to nearby cities, and even as far as California, to work in defense-related industries.

If anything, the war probably accelerated the decline of small communities in the area, since during the 1940s the county lost population even more rapidly than it had during the Depression. By 1950, when only 38,853 people lived in the area—a loss of another seven percent since 1940—the population was about the same as it had been in 1900. Many of the communities in the county lost their schools in the years during and just after the war, including Brushy (1945), Jackson (1945), Mager (1945), Type (1945), Concord (1946), Conoley (1946), Fairview (1946), Gravel Hill (1946), Lawler (1946), Beaukiss (1947), Hare (1947) Rock House (1947), and Alligator (1948).

Top, left: Dorothy Fisher, eighteen, riding a longhorn bull on Elzie Fisher's farm near Florence.

COURTESY OF THE WILLIAMSON COUNTY HISTORICAL COMMISSION AND LESTER FISHER.

Top, right: The Thrall High School Girl's Basketball team in 1945.

COURTESY OF THE WILLIAMSON COUNTY HISTORICAL COMMISSION AND MARGRET MCCARN.

Bottom: Donald and Larry Rydell rolling cotton in the 1940s.

COURTESY OF THE WILLIAMSON COUNTY HISTORICAL COMMISSION AND LARRY RYDELL.

By the late 1940s the county's vastly improved road network had helped to create an urbanizing trend and made further school consolidations not only palatable but possible. After the state legislature passed a series of school reforms known as the Gilmer-Aiken Laws in 1949, school consolidations in Williamson County rapidly accelerated. In 1949, the communities of Barker, Bell, Berry's Creek, Ranger Branch, Sandoval, Tennill, Theon, Walnut Spring, Waterloo, and Woodrow lost their schools. In 1950, the list grew to include Beyersville, Lawrence Chapel, Rice's Crossing, Turkey Creek, Union Chapel, Walburg, and Weir. Siloam (1951), Schwertner (1954), and Hare (1957) soon followed.

The county's children would receive better educations than in the old schoolhouses, but many communities had lost the central symbols of their existence. Centralization in pursuit of efficiency had transformed farming practices and was still pushing tenant farmers and sharecroppers off the land; now, in educational reforms, it was helping to break down old communities already weakened by population loss. A way of life was fading away, memorialized mainly by hundreds of abandoned houses scattered across the landscape.

The historic drought of the 1950s, which lasted for about seven years, finally convinced a number of other farmers to move on; at about the same time, the widespread adoption of cotton-picking machines eliminated demand for that kind of labor. Almost 195,000 acres were planted in cotton in 1950; in 1959, only about 94,000 were. By that time there were only 2,587 farms left in the county, a little more than half the number in 1930. Only 940 tenants and sharecroppers remained, and the county's population had dwindled to 35,044.

The area's African-American population had been dropping off since the Depression, as

Above: Cotton Beauty Flo Kroger, sixteen, Fourth of July beauty queen in a cotton field near Taylor, 1946.
COUTESY OF THE WILLIAMSON COUNTY HISTORICAL COMMISSION AND FLO THOMPSON.

Right: "Cowgirl:" Madge McCormick Smith in the Florence/Andice area during the 1950s.
COURTESY OF THE WILLIAMSON COUNTY HISTORICAL COMMISSION AND MADGE MCCORMICK SMITH.

Top: A pickup of celebrants representing the Catholic Daughters of America in a parade in Taylor, c. 1940s.

COURTESY OF THE TAYLOR PUBLIC LIBRARY.

Middle: A group of Mexican Americans harvesting onions in the 1940s. The truck belonged to Lorenzo Camacho.

COURTESY OF THE WILLIAMSON COUNTY HISTORICAL COMMISSION AND DANIEL C. CAMACHO.

Bottom: Helen Howland at her baby shower in Georgetown, January 1953.

COURTESY OF THE WILLIAMSON COUNTY HISTORICAL COMMISSION AND CONNIE KANETSKY.

Louis Kroger with a catfish he caught in Brushy Creek near Rice's Crossing, 1956.

COURTESY OF THE WILLIAMSON COUNTY HISTORICAL COMMISSION AND FLO THOMPSON.

sharecroppers and others had pulled up their roots and looked for opportunities elsewhere. The Census had counted 7,056 blacks in Williamson County in 1930; by 1960, when all but 4,878 had left, they accounted for about eleven percent of the area's total population. Burney Downing, a farmer in the Coupland area, noticed their shrinking numbers in his corner of the county in the years after the Depression and saw it as a significant sign of the county's transition to a different way of life. After "the machine replaced the mule," he wrote, "they [the blacks] seemed to have vanished somewhat like the Indians who long ago disappeared along the Natchez trace."

There is little or nothing left of many of the small communities that once dotted Williamson County's landscape. A traveler driving west down the Andice Road from Georgetown, for example, might notice the old Rocky Hollow cemetery, but would almost certainly miss the crumbling remains of the church where, not so long ago, hundreds of people sometimes gathered for revival meetings. Other small communities, like Schwertner, still hang on, though much reduced in size.

Top: Dr. James Lee Dickey with his wife, Magnolia, and his son, James, Jr., in Taylor. Dr. Dickey earned a national reputation during the 1950s for his medical work and his achievements as a leader of Taylor's black community.

COURTESY OF THE WILLIAMSON COUNTY HISTORICAL COMMISSION AND LESLIE HILL.

Middle: Dr. Dickey's medical clinic in the 1950s.

COURTESY OF THE TAYLOR PUBLIC LIBRARY.

Bottom: The football team of Georgetown's Carver High School, taken in 1962 before the city's schools were integrated.

COURTESY OF THE WILLIAMSON COUNTY HISTORICAL COMMISSION AND LESTER FISHER.

Top: Part of the congregation of Granger's First Baptist Church poses in the 1950s.

COURTESY OF THE WILLIAMSON COUNTY HISTORICAL COMMISSION AND MARY LOUISE ARRINGTON BIRKELBACK.

Bottom: Iola Bowden Chambers, the director of Georgetown's Negro Fine Arts School, with E. J. Johnson and Margie Nell Johnson. The school operated for almost twenty years before it closed in 1965, as the Georgetown school system became integrated.

PHOTO BY EVANS STUDIO, GEORGETOWN. COURTESY OF MARY ELIZABETH FOX.

Longhorns rumble past the Williamson County Courthouse in Georgetown March 1998 as part of the county's sesquicentennial celebration that year.

COURTESY OF JOHN J. LEFFLER.

Into a New Era

In the 1960s, even as Williamson County's old cotton culture was fading away, a new kind of society was emerging in the area, and county residents began to witness dramatic changes in race relations and other patterns of living. Supreme Court decisions and federal legislation restored the civil rights of the area's blacks; by 1968 all of the county's schools were integrated, and African-Americans, now able to vote, began to have more influence in county politics, especially in Taylor. The county's Mexican-American population continued to grow after 1960; by 1990, they were the largest ethnic group in the county. Meanwhile farm and ranch families, equipped with televisions and modern electrical appliances, lived much more comfortably than only thirty years before and were more closely connected to patterns of life and thought that shaped the entire nation. The completion of Interstate Highway 35 in the early 1960s also began to change how and where people in the county worked, shopped, and lived. After declining for more than thirty years, the county's population increased again in the 1960s, rising to 37,305 by 1970.

In the late 1970s boarded-up buildings in Georgetown's sleepy central business district still reflected the county's long economic decline. In 1976, though, a reawakening of interest in the city's history and heritage was sparked by observances of the national Bicentennial. That year, thanks to the efforts of local citizens, the city's Courthouse Square was entered into the National Register of Historic Places, and the Georgetown Heritage Society was established. By the early 1980s a number of people had begun to appreciate the potential of the surviving High Victorian commercial architecture around the Square. Laura Weir-Clarke, a Georgetown native who had majored in architectural design at the University of Texas, and her family purchased the historic Steele Store-Makemson Hotel building on the corner of Eighth Street and Austin Avenue and began to restore it. In 1981 she also planned and produced the first

❖

Above: The Andice General Store was built in the 1890s and has been run for many years by the Davidson family. It once served as the town's post office and was still the local "shopping mall" for townspeople in the year 2000.

COURTESY OF JOHN J. LEFFLER.

Below: The John Atkinson store in Florence, the town's first general store, was built in 1854 by Henry Dixon Love and Columbus "Lum" Backman. The building's first floor was used to harbor livestock; the store operated on the second level; and the Atkinson family lived on the third floor. The stone for the structure was taken from a quarry at Gravel Hill, about five miles away, and carried to the site by wagon. Each trip took more than a day.

COURTESY OF JOHN J. LEFFLER.

Christmas Stroll on the Square. Meanwhile Genevieve Atkin was working to enroll Georgetown in the Main Street Program, which provided tax exemptions and other incentives to encourage the restoration of buildings and economic development. In 1982, with the support of the city and county governments and a number of local citizens, Georgetown was designated a Main Street City. By 1984, forty restorations had been completed, and the city was beginning to enter its second "Golden Age."

The spirit of civic activism associated with the Main Street Program had also created a greater awareness of other needs in the Georgetown community and led to the creation of several community service agencies. Handcrafts Unlimited, a non-profit shop selling items made by area artists and artisans aged fifty and over, opened its doors on the Square in the historic Booty Building on Eighth Street. The Caring Place, another social service agency, also had its origins in this era of civic dynamism, and others soon followed.

In the 1970s the growth of nearby Austin had begun to spill north into Williamson County. In the 1980s and 1990s, as development crept and then raced up I-35 and State Highway 183, Georgetown, Round Rock, Cedar Park, and Leander grew exponentially. Round Rock attracted its first high-tech industry, Westinghouse, in the mid-1970s and another, DuPont Photomask, in 1986. In 1994, Dell Computer Corporation, now the world's largest manufacturer of personal computers, established its corporate headquarters in Round Rock; by 1999 more than fifty technology companies, employing about 16,000 people, were doing business in the city. Round Rock became one of the fastest-growing communities in America, and new stores, restaurants, and housing developments seemed to

sprout up everywhere. Fewer than 3,000 people lived in Round Rock in 1970; by 1999, its population had grown to over 53,000.

During the 1980s and 1990s the western part of Williamson County, especially Leander and Cedar Park, also experienced explosive growth. As late as 1990, fewer than 3,500 people lived in Leander; by 2000, about 12,000 people did. Cedar Park's population rose from 5,161 to almost 25,000 during the same period. Overall the number of people living in the county grew from 37,305 in 1970 to 85,700 by 1980; to 138,551 by 1990; and to about 220,000 by 2000. In the late 1990s, development began to run east of Round Rock down State Highway 79 toward Hutto and Taylor. By 1999 Taylor had also become a Main Street City; only a year later, several renovations had already been completed, a number of others were being planned, and the city's residents looked optimistically to the future.

At the beginning of the twenty-first century, agriculture still remained the single most important element of Williamson County's economy, but hammered by a series of drought years and low prices, many of the area's ranchers and farmers were struggling to stay in business. Already a number of ranches in the southern and western sections of the county had been subdivided for housing developments and five-acre "ranchettes," and many ranchers and farmers stayed on their lands primarily because of their love for the land and their respect for tradition.

Williamson County was moving into a new era of its development, unfolding in tandem with a growing appreciation for the parts of the county's life that were fading away. It was an accident of history—or was it?—that when, in April 2000, the first pitch was thrown in Round Rock's new Dell Diamond Baseball Stadium, the Old Settlers Park was right next door.

Above: Christ Lutheran Church still towers over the landscape between Taylor and Noack, testimony to the many farm families who once lived in the area.

COURTESY OF MARTHA MITTEN ALLEN.

Below: The Beef Club building, built in Theon, about eight miles northeast of Georgetown. The Beef Club enabled neighboring families to slaughter cattle collectively to avoid wasting meat. The club was disbanded in 1942, but the building was still standing in 2000.

COURTESY OF JOHN J. LEFFLER.

Sources

Anyone interested in Williamson County's history has to consult Clara Scarbrough's *Land of Good Water: A Williamson County History*. (Georgetown: Williamson County Sun Publishers, 1973.), one of the finest Texas county histories. For those interested in learning more about the county's many communities, the book is indispensable. Mark Odintz's history of the county in *The New Handbook of Texas* (Austin: Texas State Historical Association, 1996) provides a very good overview; *The New Handbook* also includes many other useful articles about historic personages, places and Indians in the county. Other histories of the county include W. K. Makemson, *Historical Sketch of the First Settlement and Organization of Williamson County* (Georgetown, 1904), John Griffith, "Early History of Texas," "Early History of Williamson County," "The Webster Massacre," "Williamson County Courthouse Sketches," "Sketches of Early Days in Taylor" (Taylor, n.d), Jean Shroyer and Hazel Hood, comps. and eds., *Williamson County, Texas: Its History and Its People* (Nortex Press, 1985), Estell May Norville, comp., *Students' History of Williamson County* (n.d., n.p), Julia Faye Rader's typescript history in the WPA Records Survey Collection at the Center for American History, University of Texas-Austin), and *History of Texas, Together with a Biographical History of Milam, Williamson, Bastrop, Travis, Lee and Burleson Counties* (Chicago: 1893). Archeological studies about various sites around the county can be found at the Texas Archeological Research Lab, at the Pickle campus of the University of Texas-Austin.

A number of histories of the county's cities and communities have been written over the years, including J. Gordon Bryson, *The Culture of Shin Oak Ridge Folk* (Bastrop, 1985); Ruth Mantor, *Our Town: Taylor* (Taylor, 1983); Karen Thompson and Jane DiGesualdo, *Historical Round Rock, Texas* (Austin: 1985); and Martha Allen's *Georgetown Yesteryears*, a 4-volume collection of oral histories. Many other very useful histories of county communities also have been written, though a number of them appeared originally as pamphlets and can be difficult to find. The scrapbooks maintained by the Williamson County Historical Commission contain some of these, including Burney Downing's *Coupland: A Community in the Blacklands* (1976) and Effie McCleod's *Lawler Community History*. Many other good unpublished accounts dealing with historical sites and communities can also be found in the Taylor Public Library; in the historical marker files at the Texas Historical Commission in Austin; and in vertical files on the county, its communities, and various people associated with it at the Center for American History, University of Texas-Austin.

This girl was riding to school from her home outside Granger in the early 1900s.

COURTESY OF THE WILLIAMSON COUNTY HISTORICAL COMMISSION AND DOROTHY BOHAC.

Above: Les McNeese of the Round Rock/Merrelltown area fought in World War I. He poses here with an artillery round.

COURTESY OF THE WILLIAMSON COUNTY HISTORICAL COMMISSION AND FRANCES MCNEESE ARCHER.

Below: Paul and Annie Volcik dressed up in their Sunday best for this portrait taken in the early 1900s in Granger.

COURTESY OF THE WILLIAMSON COUNTY HISTORICAL COMMISSION AND GERALDINE HERSCH.

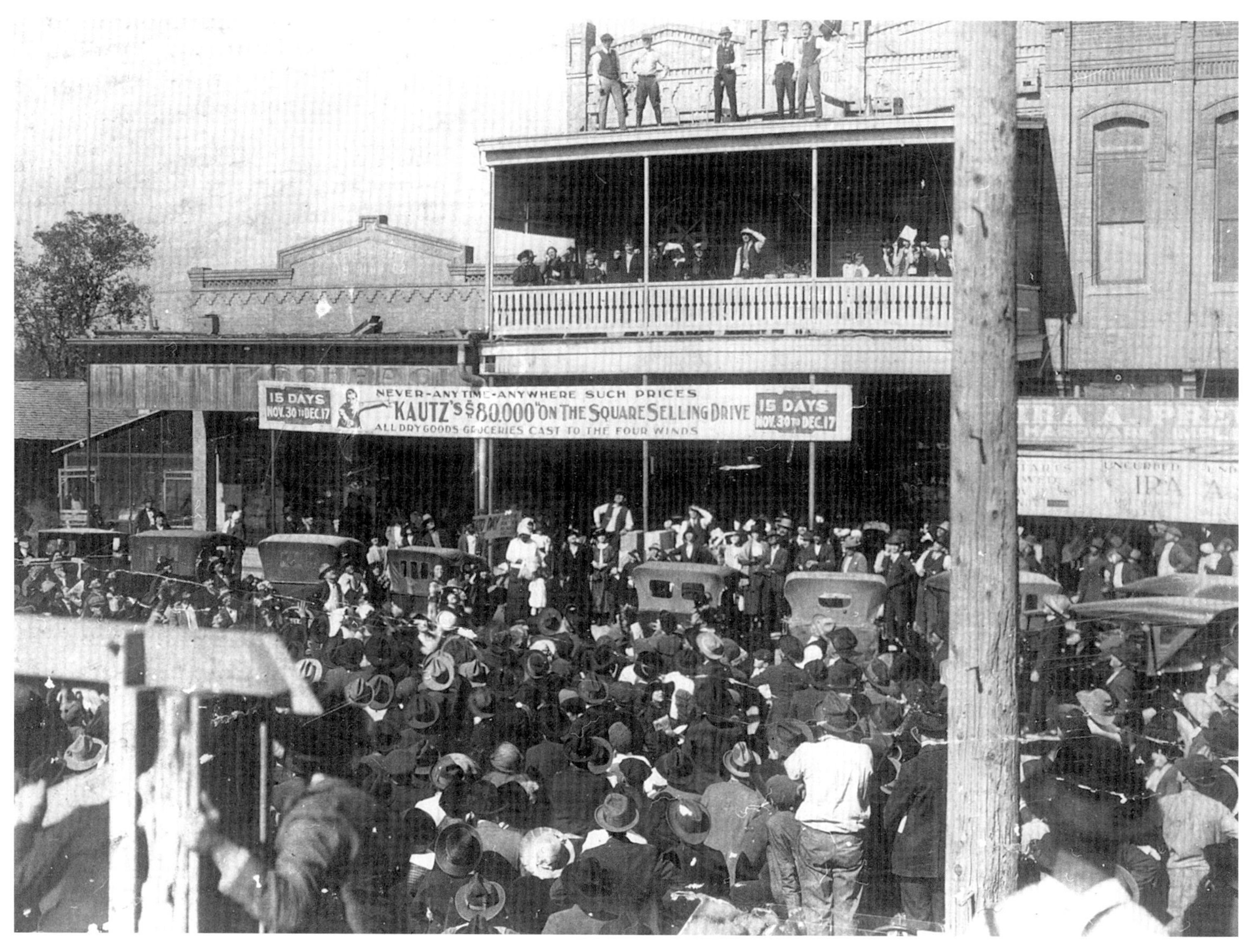

❖

A holiday crowd gathers in front of Kautz's Store during Taylor's annual Corn Festival, c. 1910s.

COURTESY OF THE TAYLOR PUBLIC LIBRARY.

Sharing the Heritage

Historic profiles of

businesses and organizations

that have contributed to

the development and the

economic base of Williamson County

Special Thanks To

The City of Taylor

Taylor Economic Development Corporation

Taylor Independent School District

Longhorn Title Company, Inc.

This is a sample caption for a photograph or illustration.

"Large enough to serve, small enough to care" is a slogan that helps to explain the success Longhorn Title Company, Inc. has enjoyed for over twenty-five years. With its main offices located on the southeast corner of the historic square in Georgetown, the company has earned a respected presence in Williamson County, providing title services for real estate transactions throughout the area.

Joe B. Long, his wife Donna, and Claude Hays originally established Longhorn Title Company in Georgetown on February 22, 1972. The company's first office was located at 711 Main; four employees performed the work. In 1978, the company purchased the historical Dimmitt Building at 801 Main, allowing the company to grow as well as maintain a location on the square. In 1983 Joe Long sold his ownership percentage to Southern Title, which is now Fidelity National Title. In 1997 Fidelity was sold to Judy Ballard, Mike Cumberland, and David Hays, making Longhorn one of a small number of independently owned and home-operated title companies. As demand for title services increased throughout the county, Longhorn Title has increased its offices, adding locations in Round Rock and Taylor. Today four locations and thirty-two employees serve the customers of Longhorn Title Company, Inc.

The buildings that house the title offices—all, incidentally, located on Main Street in their respective communities—have interesting pasts of their own. The Dimmitt Building, with its commanding presence on the southeast corner of the Georgetown Square, was built in 1901 by P. H. Dimmitt and Co., intended for use as a hotel. However, it functioned instead as a mercantile store as well as a meeting place for families and friends from the Williamson County community. Later uses included Georgetown's first movie house, an automobile agency, a drug store, a dental office, and a bus depot. Georgetown Savings and Loan Association remodeled the building in 1960. The restoration preserved the native stone Spanish arches, columns, and turrets. In 1965 the building was officially recorded as a Texas Historic Landmark. This building now functions as the headquarters for Longhorn Title Company.

Another historic building, located at 105 East Main in Round Rock, is part of the Longhorn Title family. Built in 1876 on land owned by William Cade and Joseph Lockett, the building was bought in 1883 by Dr. J. H. Johnson, who operated a paint and drug store, later adding stationery and other goods. Dr. Johnson ran the business until 1907, when S. A. Pennington opened a jewelry store. Since 1909 the building has served as a pool hall, a dry goods and grocery store, a restaurant, a furniture and appliance store, and finally, from 1986 till 1994, as Behren's Appraisal. Longhorn Title Company has called it home since 1995.

The third historic building, also located on Main Street in Taylor, has its own interesting past. House Jewelers, occupants of the building for many years, kept its valuables in a safe located inside a solid masonry room. Longhorn Title has conducted business in that office since 1997.

Local ownership allows for active interest in and support of the local communities. As a good neighbor in the business community, Longhorn Title Company is involved in the Chamber of Commerce organizations in each of the towns where an office is maintained. The company's employees volunteer with the March of Dimes, Heartwalk and the River Haven Nursing Home. In addition, numerous local civic and school organizations receive support from Longhorn Title Company.

Longhorn
Title
Company, Inc.
601 MAIN

City of Cedar Park

The railroad heritage of Central Texas survives in Cedar Park, which is home to the Austin Steam Train Association. The restored steam engine towing vintage coach cars books regular tours through the Hill Country and is an extremely popular way to view the area's spring wildflowers.

COURTESY OF AUSTIN STEAM TRAIN ASSOCIATION.

George and Harriet Cluck probably would not recognize Cedar Park in the year 2000. The community where they settled and worked during the second half of the nineteenth century has transformed from a sleepy stop on the stagecoach line to a city faced with the challenge of managing its rapid growth. Cedar Park has the distinction of being one of the fastest-growing cities in the United States. Its beginning was not filled with nearly as much promise.

Scholars believe that primitive man may have passed through the Cedar Park region about 10,000 years ago and evidence of Spaniards' entrance into the area traces back to around 1690.

Above: During the building of the State Capital in the late 1880s massive blocks of cut granite were hauled from the quarry at Granite Shoals to Austin by rail. A train wreck caused several large blocks to be dumped into Brushy Creek, where they have remained intact and undisturbed just as they fell.

COURTESY OF DUANE SMITH.

Below: One of the older ranches still in family ownership is the Fritz Robinson Ranch. The land has been in the Robinson family for over a hundred years and is the site of the one-story dwelling seen in this picture. The structure is estimated to have been built in the 1920s to house sharecroppers working on the Robinson Ranch.

COURTESY OF DUANE SMITH.

Indians who lived in Williamson County included the Tonkawa, Lipan Apaches, and the Penateka Comanches. There were also other, less populous tribes. However, the legitimate settlement of the community did not occur until the early 1870s when the Clucks arrived. They arrived nearly forty years after a blockhouse and a fort located two miles north of the current Cedar Park had been built by Texas Rangers to protect the hardy souls who ventured into the territory.

These structures had long since been abandoned and then burned by Indians when George Cluck, following a successful cattle drive in 1873, bought a ranch located on land that is the present site for Cedar Park. In 1874 his wife Harriet became the post-mistress of the community, which at that time was known as Running Brushy. Ranching was the major occupation. Water was hauled from Running Brushy Green to nearby Bagdad (later known as Leander) to supply a steam mill. A stage line from Austin to Lampasas provided the first commercial transportation in Williamson County. The route traveled through the Cluck property, and George Cluck provided fresh horses for the stage. By 1882 the railroad had found a need to lay tracks to Burnet, by way of Running Brushy. The State Capitol had burned to the ground in 1881, and the new structure was to be built of native pink granite, which had to be transported from Burnet. When the railroad came through the Cluck property, officials characteristically insisted on renaming the community to honor a railroad official, a man named Brueggerhoff. The town benefited significantly from the business generated by the hauling of 15,700 carloads of granite. As the community began to experience growth, the Clucks donated land and a building that became known as Running Brushing Community School. It was used jointly as a school and a church. By 1887 the town's official name changed to Cedar Park. During this time, Indian attacks had subsided sufficiently that more and more settlers began to occupy the community. In

1892 a store was built along the railroad tracks and was operated by the Clucks' son Emmett. That same year Cluck sold for one dollar a portion of his property adjoining the railroad, stipulating that one-half acre of the land is used as a park. The park provided an interesting picnicking destination for Austinites riding the train out to Cedar Park in search of entertainment. By 1897 a quarry opened, and Cedar Park became the heaviest freight loader between Austin and Llano, providing the only source of shell stone in the United States. The San Jacinto Monument near Houston was constructed with stone from Cedar Park. In addition to the transport of limestone, the cedar trees that were so prominent in the area provided a revenue-producing industry. The trees provided fence posts, heating fuel, rope (from the bark), cooking seasonings (from the berries), and furniture oil polish.

The first part of the twentieth century was characterized by a lack of growth. Cedar Park's population in 1906 was 200. It dropped to 100 by 1936 and rose to only 125 in 1940.

The development of the community did not begin in earnest until the 1970's. With Austin beginning to grow and transportation routes increasing in sophistication, commuting to the city from Cedar Park became a realistic possibility. City leaders in Austin looked with interest toward the Cedar Park area for annexation purposes. Residents of Cedar Park

A protective fence surrounds the McRae Family Cemetery where the early pioneer family established a farm in 1874. The cemetery was the final resting place for several family members, including Murdock McRae, his wife Isabelle Monroe McRae, their son Daniel, and at least two of Daniel's children.

COURTESY OF DUANE SMITH.

took matters into their own hands, voting overwhelmingly to incorporate. Thus Cedar Park finally became incorporated in 1973 and was designated a home rule city after voters adopted the charter in 1987. An incident in 1977 involved Austin's contention that Cedar Park's southern boundary encroached on the larger city's extraterritorial jurisdiction. A joint settlement resulted in Cedar Park's moving its southern boundary about one mile north in exchange for other land from Austin.

The 1980s and 1990s have seen population numbers continue to rise each year. The economic downturn of the mid- to late 1980s that faced many Texas cities forced Cedar Park to compete with other communities its size for continued economic security. Having survived , Cedar Park is now poised on the brink of an economic boom. Projections suggest that by 2010 Cedar Park's population will rise to 61,500, more than double the population in 1998. The growth and projected increases create challenges that city leaders strive to meet. A Comprehensive Plan is in place as a blueprint for changes and improvements that will support the city's vision of Cedar Park as a safe, family-oriented, business-friendly community offering a high quality of life for all citizens. The goal is to develop Cedar Park into an economically sustainable city that is home to families, host to business, and gateway to recreation.

To aid in the achievement of this goal, the Comprehensive Plan states objectives that reflect the expected concerns that all cities share: land use, economic development, transportation, infrastructure, and design and image. The Downtown Partnership Plan is different, however.

One of the challenges faced by city leaders was to change the image of Cedar Park as a city with a haphazardly created business district to a city with a focus. City leaders envision an entirely new Town Center that will create a sense of place for residents. The proposed Town Center will be a place where residents can live, work, shop, and play—all within the space of a master-planned downtown area. It is believed that having a vibrant, centralized downtown area in which residents can take pride will not only increase quality of life for residents but also be an attractive inducement for businesses and industries considering locating in Cedar Park.

❖

Local commercial and retail developments, such as The Railyard, frequently adopt a rail or hill country motif to recognize the importance of the railroad in central Texas growth.

COURTESY OF DUANE SMITH.

The strategies for economic development have been formulated to take into account both the desire to diversify the economy and the concern for maintenance of a desirable quality of life. Claiming that the city is a viable location for clean, technology-based industries, Cedar Park officials have set their sights on those types of enterprises. Their claim was validated when Sulzer Biologics made the decision to locate in the La Jaita Business Park. The partnership between Cedar Park and the bio-medical firm will no doubt attract the attention of other companies.

City of Georgetown

Tourists are drawn to the historic square and the shopping opportunities of downtown Georgetown, while newcomers are attracted to the small-town way of life and the good schools. Longtime residents of Georgetown have witnessed an evolving community as change and challenges have tested the leaders of the city. Throughout its history, this city—located in what is now one of the fastest-growing counties in the United States—has not stood still and allowed change and growth to dictate its character. Georgetown has chosen instead to maintain a respectful reverence for the past while facing the future with grace.

Georgetown was founded in 1848 and named county seat of Williamson County that same year. At that time the "town" was little more than an undeveloped tract overlooking the bank of the San Gabriel River to the north. Founding father George Washington Glasscock donated 173 acres of land, which was quickly surveyed and marked off in a uniform grid of lots and blocks; these were offered for sale at a public auction on July 4, 1848. This grid system of development, with a central public square donated for governmental purposes, is typical of county seats throughout the state.

Several catalysts helped shape the growth of Georgetown in the second half of the nineteenth century. It was not until 1857 that a courthouse stood in its designated central location. Official county business was originally conducted beneath an oak tree two blocks southeast of the Square, at the intersection of Ninth and Church Streets. In 1867 the first major cattle trail leading north to join the famous Chisholm Trail was routed through Georgetown. The last two decades of the nineteenth century brought great and lasting changes to the appearance of Georgetown. It was a time of vigorous economic development activity and physical expansion. Having been established as the home of Southwestern University in the late 1870s and being tied into a rapidly expanding railroad network in 1878, the county seat of Williamson County appeared to have a promising future. Downtown buildings either underwent

Above: Williamson County Courthouse, 1919.

Right: "First Monday" Trade Day.

improvements or were replaced by fine Victorian structures. Most of the downtown buildings existing today were built during this period. This robust Victorian era left its mark on the city.

A flood in 1921 not only destroyed homes, bridges, and railroads but also resulted in the deaths of one hundred people. The devastation did have a positive consequence, as dams were consequently built on Central Texas rivers, offering protection to citizens and property. District Attorney Dan Moody's successful prosecution of Ku Klux Klan members also characterized the '20s. The growth trend resumed in 1930, but setbacks from the Depression, World Wars I and II, and a regional drought weighed heavily on the local economy. The 1950s brought drought conditions to the area, broken by record-breaking rainfall in 1957.

During this period Georgetown's population growth was very modest, but some phenomenal changes were just around the corner. The construction of Interstate 35 through Williamson County in the early 1960s proved to be quite controversial. The Texas Highway Department route circled Georgetown. Leaders feared that circumventing U. S. Highway 81 would be disastrous but were proven wrong. Another significant change was the development of Lake Georgetown by the Army Corps of Engineers. This project was responsible for creating flood

❖

Above: Southwestern University, Texas' oldest chartered university.

Left: Founder's Park on the corner of 9th and Church Streets.

❖

Above: East side of Courthouse Square Historic District.

Below: Georgetown is the "Red Poppy Capital of Texas."

control, enhancing recreational capacity, and ensuring future water supply.

In the 1950s, '60s, and '70s, a gradual downturn in retail and commercial activity occurred as a result of nearby urban centers. An increased interest in history and historic preservation was generated by the nation's bicentennial.

By 1980-81 conditions were favorable for the Main Street Program, with the following elements in place: a growing population that envisioned a wealth of possibilities for the historic downtown, a proactive Heritage Society, and a National Register District in place which qualified property owners for the rehabilitation tax credit. Local preservationists learned of the Texas Main Street Program in the spring of 1981 and, following a series of town meetings, submitted an application with the overwhelming support of city and county governments and local citizens. Georgetown was selected as a Texas Main Street City in 1982 and was cited for its "high concentration of commercial Victorian architecture and excellent potential of economic development."

In 1997 Georgetown was named a Great American Main Street City by the National Trust for Historic Preservation, the first Texas city to win this prestigious award. Main Street has given and continues to give Georgetown a vision for the future. The program has organized and educated the community, making it economically viable again. The subsequent high visibility

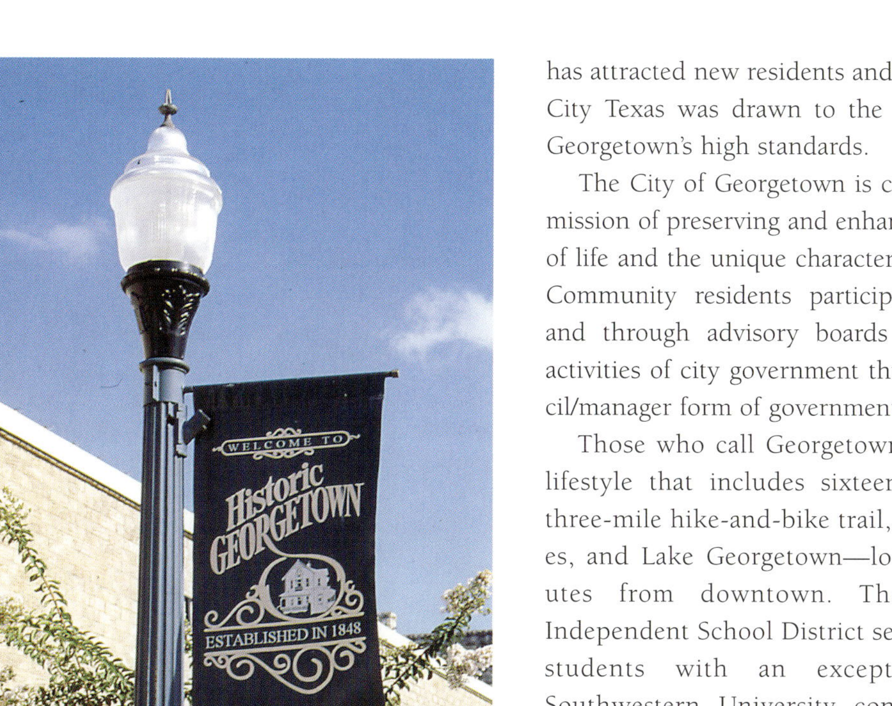

has attracted new residents and businesses. Sun City Texas was drawn to the area because of Georgetown's high standards.

The City of Georgetown is committed to the mission of preserving and enhancing the quality of life and the unique character of Georgetown. Community residents participate individually and through advisory boards that affect the activities of city government through the council/manager form of government.

Those who call Georgetown home enjoy a lifestyle that includes sixteen city parks, a three-mile hike-and-bike trail, five golf courses, and Lake Georgetown—located just minutes from downtown. The Georgetown Independent School District serves over 7,300 students with an exceptional system. Southwestern University consistently ranks high on national lists of colleges that offer superior educational experiences in a small liberal arts atmosphere.

Will growth change the character of Georgetown? Not if community leaders have their way. Long-term planning is becoming more and more a part of the government's everyday approach to managing the city. Although the community's expansion presents a challenge, leaders are committed to enter the new millennium with a clear vision. Citizens take great pride in the good life in Georgetown.

❖

Left: Georgetown was the 1997 Great American Main Street winner.

Below: A downtown festival.

City of Leander

In 1990 travelers passing through Leander might have taken note of the population sign (3,400) and the sparse number of options for stopping to eat or gas up a vehicle. Unless they had specific business in the area, they probably would have kept driving–completely unaware of the virtual explosion that was simmering just below the surface. The year 2000 presents a far different picture with the promise of more to come. Good things, that is. The population has more than tripled, and city officials find themselves scrambling to keep up with the growing needs of residents of the once sleepy town. Leander is on the rise!

In order to appreciate the Leander of today, it is essential to look at the town's beginnings. Originally called Bagdad, the town that would later become Leander was located a mile west of its current site. In the 1830s and 1840s the first permanent settlers arrived, claiming bounty land grants received in exchange for service in the Texas Revolution. By the time Texas became a state in 1845, veterans of the Texas War of Independence had built at least three log cabins. These cabins belonged to the families of Tom Hornsby, Harold Smeltzer, and James Rice. The abundance of available water and timber attracted the settlers to the area, but control of the territory did not come easily. The Texas Rangers were called in to protect the inhabitants against Indian attacks. These attacks occurred frequently and were successful, in part, due to information fed to the Indians by angry Mexicans, intent on exacting revenge for their loss in the war. The Rangers built one of the first buildings in what is now Williamson County. The building was a blockhouse that housed sixty men who protected the whites in the region. If not for so many attacks, Bagdad would probably have been inhabited earlier than the 1845 date generally attributed to its beginning.

Nonetheless, by the 1850s the town was flourishing. In 1854, Charles Babcock surveyed the town; soon after, businesses opened and, while farms were the mainstay of the area, a town with a nucleus also came into being. In spite of its isolated location, the town was somewhat progressive, boasting a cabin with puncheon floors. Whereas most of the town's buildings had dirt floors, Harold Smeltzer's cabin floors were made of split logs hewn and laid together. Another progressive aspect of the town was a "wayside inn" operated by Charles Babcock. Located on the military road between Austin and Fort Cragan (now Burnet), the town became a favorite camping place for army officers; Robert E. Lee is reported to have stayed once at Babcock's inn.

During the Civil War, large numbers of the community's men joined their southern compatriots in the war effort. At the end of the war, they were eager to return to Bagdad in order to rebuild the farms and lives they had previously enjoyed. By the early 1880s, the rail industry expanded into Texas, bringing with it plans to build tracks right through Bagdad's downtown area. Fearful that the railroad would disrupt their peaceful lifestyle, the citizens adamantly opposed the plan. Railroad officials accommodated the wishes of the residents of Bagdad by building the tracks instead one mile east of the town. Soon after the railroad had been completed, the town's businessmen and farmers realized the importance of the railroad's location and the stimulus it could provide for their shops and businesses; they decided to move the town next to the tracks. Since the railroad gave the town the reason for its location, railroad officials requested that the town be named for one of the men responsible for seeing the line completed. His name was Leander "Catfish" Brown. The town of Leander was officially created on July 17, 1882, when the railroad company sold lots, most of the remaining Bagdad residents quickly moved.

During the remainder of the nineteenth century, Leander became a community where people with traditional values lived. The town consisted of both businesses in town and large community farms. During the 1880s, the cedar post business developed into a profitable industry; although some posts were sold in Leander, most were shipped out on the railroad. Even with Leander's close proximity to the state capitol of Texas, the citizens were firmly rooted in their agricultural and rural values and ways of life. Churches became an integral part of community life, serving as centers of both worship and everyday activities for the residents. Other evidence of the churches' value to the community could be seen in emergency situations, such as the Methodist church's offer of its facilities to hold classes when a fire destroyed the community school. The education that Leander and Bagdad children received during the second half of the nineteenth century took place in various makeshift locations and was frequently taught by religious leaders. It was 1893 before the first public school was founded; in 1899 application

was made to the State of Texas to create a school district. Once established, the Leander public school became the nucleus of the community.

The first half of the twentieth century found Leander continuing to be mostly a rural community, its residents content to maintain their commitment to a basic lifestyle that placed the work ethic at the very core of its existence.

The explosion of growth that currently characterizes Leander must have many of the residents accustomed to the rural lifestyle scratching their heads in wonder. The spurt has not been without its pleasant side effects, however. City Manager Jake Krauskopf was told, shortly after he arrived in Leander, that one of his first orders of business needed to be dealing with the city-run golf course at Crystal Falls. It had become a drain on the taxpayers, so he was instructed to either "turn it around or sell it." That was in 1999, and today Crystal Falls is not only profitable but will soon be surrounded by beautiful homes in an upscale residential community currently under development. The rapid growth has provided new challenges as city leaders search for new ways of providing city utilities and services. Plans have been made to give the central part of town a new look, expanding what is already in place and building new facilities to provide for the community's needs. From hospitals to grocery store chains to property developers, business and industry are appearing at Leander's doorstep, wanting to be a part of this city that is clearly on the upswing. Leander Independent School District, which serves the children of the community, is in a building phase that does not show signs of slowing down anytime soon. It appears that the sky is the limit, as land surrounding Leander to the east, west, and north—not yet incorporated—seems to offer immense possibilities.

Quite a change for the little town that wasn't sure it wanted the railroad invading its privacy.

City of Round Rock

❖

Above: Downtown Round Rock in the pre-World War II era was a center of social activity, featuring restaurants and dry goods stores.

Below: Downtown Round Rock today is a beautifully landscaped, pedestrian-friendly historic area, home to many service businesses as well as City Hall and the public library.

Turning points—those defining moments after which nothing seems the same—can either set people back or propel them forward. A timeline of Round Rock's history reveals a series of such points, and the outcome of those events reveals the character of the people who have inhabited the area through the years. Once a sleepy little settlement that sprang up along the banks of Brushy Creek, Round Rock now stands as a prosperous city, still growing and poised confidently to enter the twenty-first century as an example of a complete community.

It started more than one hundred years ago. A large round rock in the middle of Brushy Creek signified to travelers a safe place to ford the creek. As more and more people utilized the crossing, a community developed; it became known as Brushy. In 1854 Postmaster Thomas Oatts was asked to choose a new name because another community had already selected Brushy. On August 24, 1854, the town officially became Round Rock, a name chosen for Oatts' favorite fishing hole. The years that followed brought more changes to the community. In 1864 the trail that had previously been known as the Shawnee Trail became part of the larger Chisholm Trail, a cattle trail that began in the south at the Rio Grande and extended

north to Kansas. The first cattle drive that traveled through Round Rock in 1867 created quite a spectacle, providing entertainment for many citizens of Round Rock and nearby communities. This method of transporting cattle did not last long. Progress in two forms contributed to the decline of the traditional cattle drive. In 1873 barbed wire was invented, restricting access to trails. In addition, by the early 1870s, railroads began to become prevalent as a mode of transportation. By 1876 the International and Great Northern Railroad arrived in Round Rock, having purchased land to the east of the town's commercial area, precipitating the relocation of many businesses to what is now known as the downtown business district. This move has been cited by some as "the most significant event" in its history, changing the face of Round Rock forever. A couple of years after the arrival of the railroad, another significant event took place: the shootout that resulted in the death of Sam Bass. The killing of the notorious bandit put Round Rock on the map. Although the fame had not been sought, it did provide Round Rock with a distinguishing feature. Legend and lore disagree on the exact truth of the Sam Bass story, but enough versions exist to keep the story alive even today. Throughout all of the changes, Round Rock managed to survive.

Fast-forward to present-day Round Rock, where changes have occurred at an even faster pace. Leaders of the community had the foresight to impose a zoning ordinance in 1969 and growth since that time has skyrocketed. Round Rock's population has increased from 2,811 in 1970 to 12,740 in 1980; the population grew to 30,923 in 1990, and current numbers estimate

Above: Round Rock history changed forever in the mid-1990s when Dell Computer, one of the world's leading computer companies, moved its headquarters to town.

Below: TECO-Westinghouse is Round Rock's oldest large-scale industry, having set up shop in Central Texas in the late 1970s to build industrial motors.

❖

The city's namesake marked a safe crossing of Brushy Creek for early settlers.

54,000 residents. That growth has not come without challenges. In 1978 a drought caused Round Rock wells to go dry. For a short period of time, residents found themselves with very little water; construction came to a screeching halt, and no building permits were issued. An angry group of citizens, more than five hundred strong, met with city officials, expressing displeasure with their circumstances as well as their desire for a quick solution. The problem was solved when a pipeline was established, bringing water from Lake Georgetown. The crisis turned out to be a watershed event in the history of the town. Hoping to avoid future disasters, the city decided to become proactive about the future. Civic leaders vowed that Round Rock would not become just another bedroom community to Austin. Leaders established goals: they wanted a self-sufficient infrastructure, good schools and jobs, adequate medical care, and a quality of life that would entice people to live in their community. Step by step, these objectives were achieved.

A long-term planning approach addressed infrastructure needs. Steps were taken to assure both present and future water needs would be met and that other utilities would be sufficient to serve projected growth. The city annexed over 1,000 acres of land along the I-35 corridor; the property was zoned and infrastructure was constructed. These steps were a key factor in attracting industry and in making Round Rock a prototype for economic development. The strategic selection process attracted an impressive list of businesses to Round Rock. Dell Computer is the crown jewel in the collection of commercial enterprises. Others include Farmers Insurance, SEARS Teleserv, AMP Packaging, Wayne Dresser, Tellabs, Inc., Michael Angelo's, and TECO-Westinghouse. These healthy, powerful industries have impacted the economy and improved the quality of life, a fact that is evidenced by this statistic: in July 1999, although Round Rock ranked thirty-seventh in population in the State of Texas, its rank was thirteenth in collection of sales tax.

Despite the rapid progress and the booming population growth, a small town quality and a sense of community remains in Round Rock. Many of the landmarks evoke civic pride, including: Old Settler's Park at Palm Valley, with 439 acres of land devoted to providing recreational needs of the community; the historic Palm Valley Lutheran Church; the Texas Baptist Children's Home, brought to Round Rock through the efforts of Louis and Billie Sue Henna; the downtown business district with its historic atmosphere; the Round Rock Public Library, recently expanded; and the Old Town area on Chisholm Trail.

The "can-do" spirit has benefited Round Rock on many occasions. After being told the town was too small to support a YMCA, community leaders rolled up their sleeves and made it happen. The Greater Williamson County

Left: *The Round Rock City Council creates the vision and shapes policy for Central Texas' second-largest city.*

Below: *The statue of a pioneer woman will be the first of many historic sculptures in a new park being created where the Chisholm Trail passed through Round Rock at Brushy Creek.*

YMCA now thrives, offering numerous programs that enrich the lives of community families. Another time, prospective businessmen expressed concern over the lack of local medical services found in the area. Leaders reacted, recruiting diligently to bring quality medical personnel and a first-rate hospital to Round Rock. Another challenge, keeping up with increasing student population, has been gamely met by the Round Rock Independent School District. Their efforts, along with the support of the community in the form of approved bond issues, have managed to provide quality education that ranks among the best in the state.

The future looks bright for Round Rock, but no one is standing pat. Quality of life issues are being addressed. There is a Transportation Master Plan in place to solve some of the inevitable difficulties that accompany growth. The Clay Madsen Recreation Center opened July 2000, providing 46,000 square feet of recreation space, including an indoor pool. In the spring of 2000 the Round Rock Express, a AA farm team of the Houston Astros Baseball Club, occupied a state-of-the-art stadium, offering wholesome family fun to a community that has come to expect the best.

Many years ago it was the round rock that showed travelers the safe way to get from one side of Brushy Creek to the other. Today, it is people with qualities like foresight, teamwork, commitment, and pride that are paving the way for Round Rock's safe passage into the new millennium.

First Texas Bank

Customers entering the lobby of First Texas Bank's 900 South Austin Avenue location are visually drawn to the south wall. Centrally located along that wall is a large, round door that provides access to the bank vault. The gleaming steel portal–with its non-automated workings and the twenty-four bolts that encircle the door and offer an extra measure of security—provides an intriguing example of workmanship rarely found these days. In an effort to offer its customers an interesting lobby, bank officials searched for and located the door—abandoned to storage somewhere in north central Texas but in fairly good condition—and decided to refurbish and use it.

Attention to detail is a quality that sets First Texas Bank apart. Another characteristic that makes the bank special is the personal service offered by friendly, caring professionals. This service represents a tradition that began over one hundred years ago and continues today.

Despite the inevitable changes that have transpired due to automation and other technological advances, bank President E. L. Gentry points with pride to the lack of answering machines within the offices. A real person responds to each customer's call. Furthermore, all decisions are made locally. These are just some of the features that make hometown banking at First Texas Bank a delightful experience.

First Texas Bank cites 1898 as the official date for the beginning of the bank, then known as Merchants and Farmers Bank. However, journals found in the bank's storage facilities indicate that even before the bank was official, some of its founders were involved in financial dealings through a mercantile store, extending credit and holding cash deposits for store customers.

The original Merchants and Farmers Bank was housed in the old Steele building on the southwest corner of the Georgetown Square. Seven years after its inception, the state of Texas began to grant charters to banking institutions; thus, in 1905, the newly renamed Farmer's State Bank was granted charter number seventeen. It is a charter still held by the bank and is now the second oldest charter in the state of Texas.

At that time, the bank conducted its business in the Farmer's State Bank building, located on the west side of the square in the location that will be renovated to house the Williamson County Historical Society Museum. Another name change, to Citizens State Bank, occurred in 1963; at the same time the bank opened new facilities at 1111 Austin Avenue. Continuing to flourish, the bank found itself needing even

The grounds of the First Texas Bank's main location at 900 South Austin Avenue are graced by the presence of a regal live oak tree, estimated to be approximately 150 years old.

larger facilities. The present bank building, completed in November of 1979, is located at 900 South Austin Avenue.

In January 1993 Citizens State Bank became First Texas Bank, a name chosen to reflect its association with the First Texas Bancorp. Two branch locations have been added to accommodate the rapid growth in the western part of the city. The first opened in August of 1996 and is located at 5321 Williams Drive. The latest branch, opening to the public on April 7, 1997, can be found on Del Webb Boulevard.

First Texas Bank has always maintained a conspicuous presence in the community. Its employees and its resources have played important roles in such community projects as the Main Street Project, Playscape, Georgetown Industrial Foundation, and Georgetown's 150th birthday celebration. When the tornado devastated the town of Jarrell just north of Georgetown, First Texas Bank played a part in the reconstruction effort. Service organizations such as the hospital, the Caring Place, Wesleyan Homes, and others have looked to First Texas Bank for help in financing expansion projects when needed. An active participant in the Georgetown Chamber of Commerce activities as well as many other endeavors, the bank has demonstrated its commitment to Georgetown and Williamson County again and again.

First Texas Bank represents Georgetown's best qualities—growing as gracefully as possible while maintaining the personal touches that continue its connection to the community.

Above: Sun City residents enjoy convenience in banking at the newest branch office at 480 Del Webb Boulevard.

Below: The branch office located at 5321 Williams Drive accommodates a rapidly growing area of Georgetown.

Gavurnik Homes of Georgetown

Seeing a new home come together translates into the ultimate job satisfaction for John Gavurnik, founder and president of Gavurnik Homes of Georgetown. Because of his partnership with long-time friend Bill Kennedy, Gavurnik takes pleasure in providing homeowners with the home they want—complete with options often available only in custom homes. Another source of fulfillment derives from Gavurnik's efforts to not only preserve the environment but also take advantage of the land's natural amenities—ultimately providing neighborhoods that are sources of pride in their communities.

Gavurnik's love of homebuilding began during college when he worked summers for Kennedy of Kennedy Homes Limited Partnership, a well-known Chicago-area construction firm. Following college and other career forays—including tryouts for pro-football teams and a stint in teaching—Gavurnik sought to return to the more satisfying job of building homes. He contacted his former boss, and Kennedy immediately hired him as assistant superintendent. Gavurnik's responsi-bilities increased as he became project manager, production manager, and then director of construction. These jobs prepared him for a move in 1978 to the Austin area, where he worked for Nash Phillips Copus, multi-family division, gaining additional experience over the next seven years as vice-president of multi-family construction. From 1985 to 1988, Gavurnik developed single- and multi-family residences as well as retail projects in central Texas. Unfortunately, the building slump of the mid- to late-'80s forced him back to the North, specifically to the C. P. Morgan Company of Indianapolis, where he served as vice-president of construction. Anxious to return to Texas, Gavurnik again sought out his friend Bill Kennedy. As partners, in 1992, they established Gavurnik Homes Limited Partnership in association with Kennedy Properties of Texas Land Development. Headquartered in Georgetown, the company promised an uncompromising commitment to building homes that would complement the diverse lifestyles of today's sophisticated buyers while enriching communities.

Above: John Gavurnik brings a quarter of a century in construction experience to Gavurnik Homes.

Below: The attractive exteriors of Gavurnik-built homes add beauty and character to their neighborhoods.

Conducting business in Georgetown has provided certain advantages. Despite rapid growth, Georgetown still offers adequate accessibility to public officials, a feature Gavurnik values. In addition, the homebuilder is able to positively impact the community's quality of life through his roles as chairman of the Building Standards Commission and president of the Georgetown Chapter of Homebuilders. Gavurnik also serves on the board of directors for the Texas Capitol Area Builders Association.

In addition to working in Georgetown, Gavurnik and Kennedy have brought their style of homebuilding to Round Rock, Austin, Leander, Lockhart, Liberty Hill and Manor. The business has grown from construction of twenty homes in 1992 to the completion of over ninety homes in

Left: When this home in Katy Crossing was sold, Gavurnik and his associates donated their profit for projects undertaken by the Williams County Child Welfare Board.

Below: Homebuyers appreciate the open floor plans that offer easy traffic flow as well as abundant light.

1999. Gavurnik employs a full-time staff of eleven office personnel and construction supervisors while relying heavily on subcontractors. He speaks proudly of the reciprocal loyalty he and his subcontractors have established with one another. The concept of loyalty extends to his homebuyers. Gavurnik states, "I don't care if a problem crops up three years after the warranty has run out. If it's apparent that we didn't do it right the first time, then we'll fix it."

The most recent neighborhood Gavurnik Homes Limited Partnership and Kennedy Properties of Texas has developed is Katy Crossing, located in Georgetown's northeast corner. This community of homes typifies the high standards set by the two partners. One of the homes located in Katy Crossing also demonstrates Gavurnik's generous heart. For this particular project, Gavurnik—along with employees and subcontractors—donated their profit from the home's sale to the Williamson County Child Welfare Board; the sum of $16,000 provided Christmas presents for many needy children. In another act of generosity, Gavurnik's firm provided assistance in rebuilding Jarrell after the devastating tornado in 1997.

All things considered, it has been professional football's loss and Williamson County's gain that John Gavurnik decided to build his fortune in central Texas. The future looks bright as Gavurnik Homes enters the new millennium with a continued commitment to the growing business, while producing a quality product and maintaining a respect for the environment.

City National Bank of Taylor

Four generations of the Griffith family are pictured above. Chairman of the Board Ed C. Griffith, Sr. and Executive Vice President Eddie Griffith, Jr. carry on the family tradition at City National Bank in Taylor. Behind them are photographs of Ed C. Griffith's grandfather, City National Bank founder John H. Griffith, far right, and his father, John M. Griffith, center.

April 3, 2000 marked the one-hundredth anniversary of City National Bank of Taylor. Such an occasion provides the opportunity to look back and appreciate the past. It also is a time to look forward and consider the future.

The Articles of Association were signed on February 10, 1900. Signers included John H. Griffith, Dr. R. H. Eanes, J. J. Thames, C. C. Hooper, S. A. Easley, H. T. Kimbro, and Robert D. Penn. On the day the charter was issued, April 3, the capital stock was $50,000 and the bank was housed on property that is now home to the bank's lending center. In the early days, most of City National Bank's customers were involved in agriculture. A leather-bound ledger held a careful record of each day's transactions, and customers were known by names rather than by account numbers.

Through the years, City National Bank has remained close to many of its original precepts. Agriculture-related business, small businesses, and individuals continue to form an important part of CNB's customer base. The ledger, with its black and red writing pens, continued its function of recording transactions until the 1980s. Patrons of the bank can still expect to be called by name. Another tradition—initiated when John H. Griffith became part of the original group of founders—has survived. John H. Griffith served the bank first as a member of the board of directors, then as vice-president, as president for twenty-seven years, and finally as chairman of the board. His son, John M. Griffith, became president upon his father's retirement from that post. After John M. Griffith served as president, he became chairman of the board. The position of president went to his son, Ed Griffith, who serves as chairman of the board today. Eddie Griffith, Jr., the great-grandson of the founder, has returned to the bank and serves as an executive vice-president.

Adherence to tradition has not resulted in lack of growth. Quite the contrary, the bank's assets have grown to over $145 million. As the community has grown, technology has become a vital part of the bank's approach to business. One of the top technologically proficient banks in Texas, CNB was among the first to make Internet banking available for its customers. Being a one-bank holding company with mostly local stockholders allows CNB more flexibility in providing services for its customers. While all business is conducted locally, CNB prides itself on providing all services that one could find anywhere else. Plans for the future include being a financial partner with

the bank's customers, providing a total service package that will meet all financial needs.

City National Bank maintains a noticeable presence on Main Street in Taylor, occupying several city blocks. The main lobby and offices are housed in a building that was purchased after a rival bank failed to survive the economic roller-coaster of the 1980s. Next door to that Main Street structure is a building that had been purchased from the Duffy family in 1908; the former saloon received a new exterior, then served as the bank's headquarters from 1909 until 1965. Across the street from these buildings is the bank's lending center, housed on property that was expanded to include the building constructed on the bank's original site. The newest facility—the investment center—is located in a renovated building next to the lending center. Not only does the renovation of the building support the city's Main Street Project, but the separate venture it houses confirms the bank's commitment to provide a comprehensive array of services to its customers. A drive-in bank located away from the downtown area provides a convenient alternative for customers.

Holding on to what is good from the past while keeping an eye on the future—these are qualities that brought CNB through its first century and will contribute to its success in its second century of service to Williamson County.

Above: City National Bank operated from the two-story structure on the right from 1900 to 1908. The building on the left was completed in 1965 and currently houses the City National's Lending Center.

Below: City National Bank's Main Street Banking Center opened in 1995. It is adjacent to the old bank building occupied by City National Bank from 1908 to 1965. The former bank building is again owned and in use by the bank having been reacquired in 1992.

TECO-Westinghouse

Above: The site's mascots since 1972.

On the east side of I-35 at the north end of Round Rock's city limits, set back from the highway, there stands an imposing brown building guarded out front by three majestic Longhorn steers. Inside the 500,000 square-foot building is a plant that manufactures large motors that are used in the power generation, steel, petrochemical, and other industries. As companies go, this striking structure—now known as TECO-Westinghouse—has experienced its share of changes during its life in Williamson County.

In 1971 Westinghouse decided to expand operations from its manufacturing base located in Lester, Pennsylvania. After examining twenty-four possible locations across the United States, the company chose to come to Round Rock. Westinghouse officials were impressed with Williamson County, admiring the work ethic found here and favoring the area for its proximity to both a major university and an airport. The company soon initiated machine-shop training classes, and in 1972, the "first chip was turned." Gas turbines, weighing as much as 150 tons and measuring up to fifty feet in length, were manufactured. Business proceeded smoothly until the oil crunch of 1974 tripled the price of fuel, and the turbines–which could use as much as fifty-five gallons of petroleum per minute—became too impractical. That year the plant closed, reopening in 1975 as the Heavy Industrial Motor Division of Westinghouse. For a number of years, the company struggled but finally achieved a break-even point in 1984. A celebration marked the event and included a performance by fledgling come-dian Jay Leno. Even so, in December 31, 1987, the heavy motor division ceased operation; on January 1, 1988, Westinghouse Motor Company began operations as a wholly-owned subsidiary of the parent company. WMC began its association with TECO (Taiwan Electric and Machine Company) by forming a partnership in which TECO owned approximately forty percent. Production of large motors dominated the business over the course of the next few years until

March 1995, when Westinghouse sold WMC to TECO. The only remnant of Westinghouse that exists now is the use of the name as part of the company's title: TECO-Westinghouse.

The company has provided employment to numbers that have ranged from 38 to 850. During some of the years when production was down, space was leased to an array of tenants involved in, among other things, the super-collider project and Power Computing. Currently, there are approximately 600 people who make their living at TECO-Westinghouse. Besides providing employment, TECO-Westinghouse contributes to the community in several ways. Some of their involvement includes working with Easter Seals to provide employment opportunities and supporting the March of Dimes, the Blue Santa program, "Coats for Kids" and the United Way.

Originally Westinghouse acquired 3,400 acres, beginning with the purchase of the 1776 Ranch. After adjusting goals and needs, the company sold all but 116 acres. The patch of pasture in front of the building where the Longhorn steers reside has an interesting history. Initially planned as a recreation area, Westinghouse had envisioned a small pond and picnic tables that would provide an enjoyable respite for employees. However, liability concerns put a stop to the plans. Instead, the area has become home to three Longhorn steers that preside over the land with an imposing and regal presence. The three steers who currently reside at TECO-Westinghouse are numbers five, six, and seven in an elite group of carefully chosen animals. The horns of the first four can be found on display at various places inside the facility.

Today the company focuses on building motors of all sizes and taking advantage of the tremendous opportunities available in the motor drive and service areas of the business. TECO's goal is to be one of the top five producers of motors in the world. As inevitable new challenges continue to present themselves, TECO-Westinghouse looks forward to its continued association with Williamson County.

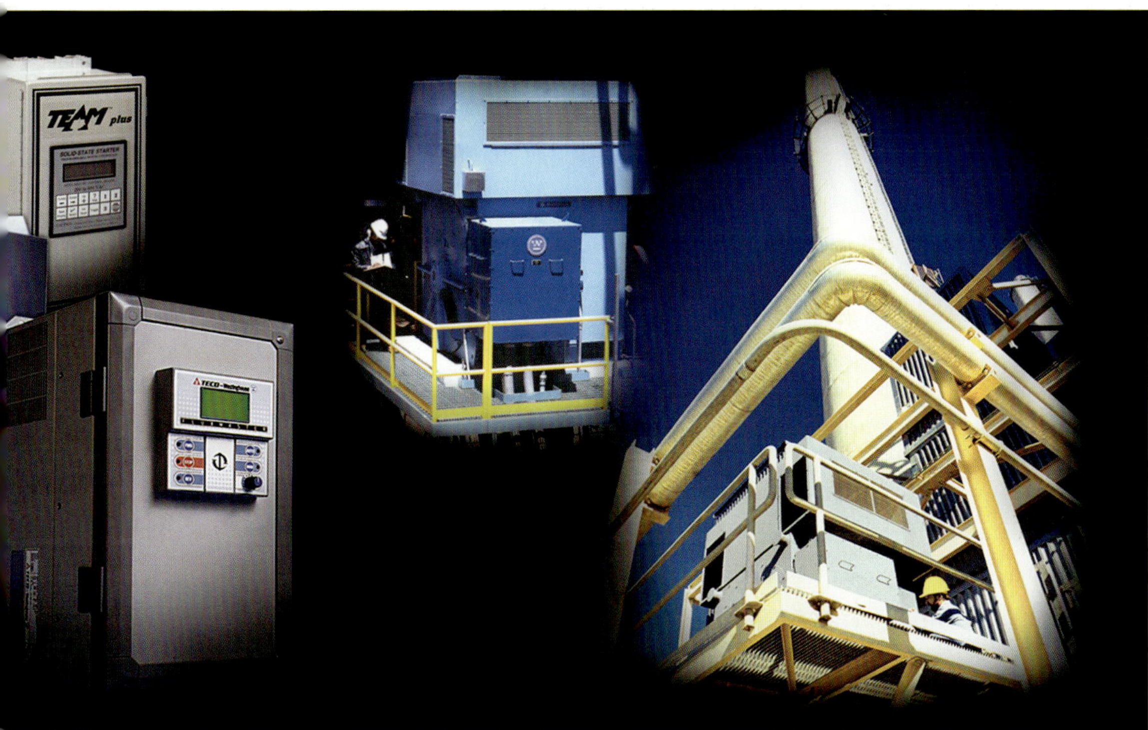

Above: Very large DC motors.

Left: From left to right: AC and DC motors, motor controls and variable-frequency drives, and service activities.

First Baptist Church of Georgetown

❖

During the 1880s, this church, located at Sixth and Church Street, was constructed on land donated by Mrs. Lizzie Glasscock Talbot. This church and a parsonage were built during the pastorate of Reverend Abram Weaver.

Early records of First Baptist Church of Georgetown indicate the formation of groups that focused on outreach programs to address needs in the community. A look at the current church body reveals a similar emphasis. One might say not much has changed, but making that assumption would be a huge mistake. The story of First Baptist Church began on October 30, 1866, when the first gathering was held. Throughout its 133-year history, the church has handled changes and challenges with commitment and courage.

Thirteen charter members answered the call from Reverend J. S. Abbott to band together and organize a Baptist church. The worshippers met in the Union Building, a school that served as a church for several denominations on Sundays. Early preachers in the church were Reverend R. H. Tabaferro and Reverend George W. Baines, Sr., the maternal grandfather of U. S. President Lyndon Baines Johnson.

The 1879 Camp Meeting at the "Fair Grounds" (now called San Gabriel Park) provided a turning point for the church. Five hundred residents from Georgetown and the surrounding communities accepted Christ at that meeting, seventy-five of them joining the First Baptist Church. The Ladies Aid Society was enthusiastically formed, followed two years later by the Young Men's Prayer Meeting. With these events, the growth of the First Baptist Church began.

In 1880, the Southern Presbyterians offered to share their building at the corner of 7th and Myrtle Streets with the Baptists on alternating Sundays. A donation of land at Church and Sixth Streets by Mrs. Lizzie Glasscock Talbot in the 1880s paved the way for a church and a parsonage to be built.

In 1894, another church, Central Baptist, was formed in the community. Ten years later, the congregation found its numbers dwindling; the remaining members requested to be united with First Baptist Church. Members agreed that both churches be dissolved for a period of twenty-four hours; the next day, with Reverend Abram Weaver moderating, the two churches became one. The actual date of the organization of the present First Baptist Church in Georgetown is 1904. This consolidation initiated an era of harmony and renewed ministry throughout the community.

The need for additional meeting space and amenities throughout the years has been met by both purchases of land and utilization of generous donations. The church facilities relocated from Sixth and Church Streets to Tenth and Main Streets in the late 1920s. Expansions in the vicinity of this building along with an early 1960s renovation of the sanctuary served the church's needs until 1987, when a satellite facility was built on Highway 29 West. The burden of holding services and events at both locations led to a Deacons' Committee recommendation that all worship services and Sunday school should be held at the west location and that the downtown property should be used "to the best interest of First Baptist Church." Following this decision, the facilities at Tenth and Main Streets were sold to a newly organized church, Main Street Baptist Church, in October of 1989.

The present-day First Baptist Church serves a congregation of 2,500-plus and again faces the challenge of providing adequate facilities. Groundbreaking ceremonies took place in November 1999, for a new Worship Center.

Just as missions provided the focus of the early church members, the church today supports numerous missionary efforts. The Acuña Mission in Mexico has been a project since 1992; church members help meet the congregation's medical, spiritual, and religious needs. In addition, the church carries out other active outreach programs, providing volunteers opportunities to serve while ministering to a broad spectrum. Among these ministries are Disciple Now, Team Kid (an after-school Bible club for apartment-dwelling community children), retreats and camps for all ages, and a host of other ministries.

Looking toward the twenty-first century, congregation members and ministers know that past challenges not only have set the standard for today but also have helped solidify a commitment to the future for the First Baptist Church.

An artist's rendering of the new First Baptist Church Worship Center. Groundbreaking ceremonies for the center took place in November 1999.

Union State Bank

❖

Union State Bank Chairman of the Board and CEO Bernie M. Beck and his wife, Sis.

In 1928 three banks—Florence State Bank, Briggs State Bank, and Farmer's State Bank—joined together to become Union State Bank. The union of the three created a strong, small-town bank able to weather the Depression. Union State Bank has been going strong ever since. In the last decade, a time when Williamson County ranked as one of the fastest growing counties in the country, USB had its own growth spurt, adding four new branches by 1997 and raising assets from $24 million to $175 million. Branches are located in Georgetown, Liberty Hill, Round Rock, and Killeen. The bank that began on Main Street in Florence now serves urban as well as rural depositors.

Original stockholders included former Briggs Bank President H. J. McGuire, M. Patterson, J. C. Wright, R. N. Watson, John Brewster, Mrs. Louie Brewster, T. M. Williams, P. A. Wales, J. P. Storey, W. A. Wilson, J. D. Howell, J. M. Smith, and W. C. Love. Brewster was the first president, succeeded shortly thereafter by Dr. O. B. Atkinson, who served for twenty-five years. In September 1955 Roy J. Smith, president of First National Bank in Killeen, and Bernie M. Beck acquired USB. Beck bought controlling interest in 1972 and currently serves as chairman of the board and CEO. "We are delighted to have four out of five banks in Williamson County. The response from citizens to our presence in the county has been outstanding. The majority of our growth has occurred over the past twenty-five years. The Killeen branch opened in 1990, expanding to a newly constructed building in 1992. Georgetown opened in 1993 and moved to a larger building in 1996. Round Rock opened in June 1997 and expanded in September 1997. Liberty Hill opened in a new building in August 1997. You can see from the rapid growth that we are serving the people of Williamson County, and we are grateful to them for their acceptance."

Beck celebrated his fiftieth year in banking in 1995. He has been deeply involved in bringing sufficient water to Williamson County, serving on a special Governor's Task Force on long-range water plans. In addition to numerous other community activities, Beck currently serves on the boards of directors for Scott & White Hospital and the University of Central Texas. Sis Beck, Bernie's wife and officer for new accounts at the Killeen branch, has her own long list of volunteer accomplishments, including the establishment of the Florence Library, which brought her national recognition, and service on the boards of directors for Central Texas College Foundation and Channel 62. The Becks' daughter, Coleen, joined the bank in 1996 and works with the bank's computer networks.

T. E. Beck, Bernie's brother, manages the main bank in Florence. He celebrated his fortieth year with USB in 1998. He has served on the Florence Chamber of Commerce and other commissions. "Having been in ranching all my life, it is tough to see the subdividing of the old 'home places.' The area growth has had a positive effect on the Florence branch's business, and we look forward to this increase. However, we will always offer 'hometown' service."

In 2000 the Becks serve as directors along with Branch Managers Dale M. Alley (Round Rock/Hutto), Charles S. Parker (Georgetown), and Randy Sutton (Killeen); Operations Manager Douglas A. Baker (Florence); Senior Vice-President J. C. Walker (Killeen); Bennie Gower (Florence); and Dr. William Roach (Killeen and Sun City, Georgetown).

The 1928 motto of "The Friendly Bank" has been modified to "Where People Make the Difference!" The current slogan reflects USB's trademark commitment to building the community from within, ensuring that money goes into projects and businesses to improve local economies. Although USB's "family" has made substantial investments in new technology and has incorporated Internet banking, the main focus remains community service and spirit. This combination offers a promising balance of "high tech and high touch" in the new millennium.

Florence State Bank and Old Mercantile Warehouse (center), which served from 1928 to 1972, is flanked by (clockwise from top) Union State Bank-Florence (1972); Union State Bank-Georgetown (1993); Union State Bank-Liberty Hill (1997); Union State Bank-Round Rock (1997); and Union State Bank-Killeen (1990).

THE OTHER CONSULTING COMPANY

The world of technology has spawned a profusion of support services. The more capabilities computers are able to provide for businesses, the more necessary it becomes to ensure that all systems operate smoothly and appropriately. Enter THE Other Consulting Company, based in Austin but active throughout the world.

Recognizing the need for his services, Lawrence Winter and his wife Rosanna, founded THE OCC in 1993. At the time the company functioned as a s-corporation, and word-of-mouth referrals kept employees busy. In January 1999 the company became a full corporation; in February a move was made from a home office to a suite of offices located at 15808 RM 620 North in Austin. An aggressive marketing campaign accompanies the growth phase that is currently underway. THE OCC employs six full-time employees and seven associates that consult for the company. Plans include adding technical staff, expert consultants, and office personnel to accommodate the growing clientele list.

❖

Above: Lawrence and Rosanna Winter, founders of THE Other Consulting Company, in 1993.

Below: Steve Zimmer, partner, and his wife, Maryann, at the fiftieth birthday party for Lawrence Winter, August 28, 1999.

A wide variety of services are offered by THE OCC to address all areas of a client's needs for management of operating software systems. One of the specialized services applies to information security. THE OCC's service might begin with a systematic review of security practices, or the client might prefer to move directly to one or more of a host of other services, including: organization and management; classification and ownership; security architecture; policies, standards, and procedures; software installation, configuration, and administration; education and training; benchmarking; and security software conversion. Another area of specialty deals with business continuity planning. THE OCC offers assistance in the following areas: business impact analysis; risk management; strategy studies; recovery plan development; continuity plan audit; training; continuity plan testing; and continuity plan maintenance. Generally speaking, no two clients present the same challenges due to the individual natures of their systems; thus, the strategies utilized in providing the appropriate services are always customized to fit specific needs. In addition, the highly trained consultants at THE OCC take care to meet the client's needs in the most effective, cost-efficient way possible.

The unique feature that enables THE OCC to offer these services is a system created by founder Lawrence Winter known as Platform Management Methodology (PMM). PMM is a highly automated installation and maintenance process that tailors systems software for its clients. The process incorporates a set of standards and procedures that allows for incorporation of software enhancements and

aids in the management of a complex MVS-driven environment. Five phases—analysis, strategy, execution, support, and audit—make up the methodology. By applying these steps to the systems software, THE OCC can determine the most effective way to provide a current and stable operating platform for a main frame.

THE OCC makes life easier for a company's workers, enabling them to focus more on their jobs and less on the tedious details of software compatibility. The company's 24-7 approach to providing maintenance and its commitment to updating systems as needed add to the value of the services. Among the clients who utilize THE OCC's consulting services are large manufacturers, hospitals, retailers, and banks.

The commitment to round-the-clock service has created some interesting twists in the schedules of Rosanna and Lawrence Winter. One client, concerned about the possibility of the Y2K catastrophe, tested the company's pledge to be available whenever needed by requiring THE OCC to be present on site during the transition from December 31, 1999 to January 1, 2000. Just as THE OCC had expected, systems performed as expected with no interruption in service.

THE Other Consulting Company has found a comfortable niche in the technological workplace. Considering the world's growing dependence on technology and the continued move to centralized offices, there is no indication that business will slow down anytime soon.

Above: Cheryl Miller, administration director, and Steve Olshefski, administrative assistant.

Bottom, left: Christine Proulx, security and systems analyst, with her sister, Cathy.

Bottom, right: Edward Olshefski, associate, and his family.

City of Taylor

❖

Above: A 1925 model American LaFrance pumper (left) and a 1916 American LaFrance ladder truck are displayed in front of the original city hall building which housed the Taylor Fire Department, c. 1925.

Below: A 1996 Pierce Saber pumper (left) and a 1999 Pierce aerial ladder truck await the call to action in front of the 1935 Taylor City Hall, which houses the Taylor Fire Department, c. 2000.

Several Central Texas towns owe their beginnings to the International and Great Northern Railway routes. Opened on June 26, 1876, Taylor Station was named to honor a railroad official; the name later changed to Taylorsville and finally became known as Taylor. From its initial population of around a thousand, Taylor now boasts 15,000 residents and seems headed toward higher numbers. Although farming and farm-related businesses have historically been the mainstay of the community's economy, Taylor's story is now taking on a new twist.

Snapshots of yesteryear chronicle Taylor's diverse roots. Hometown boy Dan Moody was the first attorney to successfully prosecute a member of the Ku Klux Klan and was elected Texas' youngest governor. Bill Pickett, a black cowboy who gained rodeo fame through his unique style of "bulldogging," hailed from Taylor and was posthumously inducted into the Cowboy Hall of Fame. During the 1920s the St. Louis Browns' professional baseball team used Taylor's baseball field as spring practice headquarters. In the mid-1920s cultural entertainment flourished with a fifty-member symphony orchestra.

The future promises to add new roots, thanks in part to the exploding high-tech industry that has inundated Austin and surrounding communities. When asked about future growth, Frank Salvato, manager of this city located thirty miles northeast of Austin, commented, "The town is going to grow. The goal is to guide the growth and plan for it without diminishing quality of life for the people who live here." The City works closely with the Taylor Economic Development Corporation to attract businesses that will contribute to a balanced economy. Named an official Texas Main Street City for 1999, Taylor is utilizing grants to support revitalization of the downtown area—restoring historical buildings and adding sidewalks, benches, pedestrian lighting, and landscaping. These efforts will honor the past while defining the future.

Cornfields and cotton still line the highways leading into Taylor, but the view inside the city limits offers new insights into the face of progress.

TAYLOR ECONOMIC DEVELOPMENT CORPORATION

In 1994 the Taylor Economic Development Corporation (TEDC) was established, thanks to a one-half-cent sales tax increase approved by voters. The organization has worked to increase business and industry revenues in order to create more skilled employment opportunities and to reduce the residential property owners' tax burden. Utilizing well thought-out strategies, the TEDC has partnered with numerous community organizations to create win-win situations that will continue to pay dividends to Taylor citizens.

A significant obstacle that the TEDC faced initially was the lack of a large, skilled workforce. Industries that otherwise found Taylor an appealing community in which to do business were concerned by this shortcoming. Seeking a solution, the TEDC worked with Temple College to establish the Taylor Learning Center to provide the training necessary to equip workers to assume the jobs created when new industry came to town. The Learning Center—established in 1996—has proven extremely successful. The result has been an increase in family income, a notable increase in business activity, and a rise in tax revenue. The presence of the college in Taylor has also raised the number of local-area high school graduates who continue their education.

Another lure to new businesses is an additional industrial park, opened in 2000. Mustang Creek Industrial Park, a TEDC-sponsored project, joins Southpark as enterprise zones that seek to attract second-tier suppliers for Texas high-tech industries. Taylor Technologies and Alliance Chemical have already located in Mustang Creek Industrial Park. It is expected that more high-tech support businesses will follow.

Numerous other projects have been initiated and supported by the TEDC during its six-year existence. The TEDC has assisted more than twenty-five companies to expand or relocate to Taylor, resulting in more than 750 jobs. Over $2 million in external grant funds have also been secured for the community.

The half-cent sales tax approved by voters for economic development has been and will continue to be a sound investment.

Above: Mustang Creek Industrial Park is a TEDC-sponsored project that is paying big dividends by attracting industries to Taylor.

Below: The study programs offered at Temple College–Taylor Center prepare students for the many new job opportunities available in the Taylor area.

Taylor Independent School District

❖

Above: Texas State Comptroller Carole Keeton Rylander helps deliver one of 290 laptops to Taylor High School freshman Cale Hall.

Below: Over 500 THS students have been "granted" laptop computers to use through graduation. Phases III and IV will see all 900 THS students receive laptops for high school use.

Ninth-grade students entering Taylor High School for the 1999-2000 school year were issued laptop computers to use for the duration of their high school years. The program, placing technology at the fingertips of students, is a reflection of the goal Taylor Independent School District has set "not only to educate students but to prepare them for the challenges and changes of the future." In Taylor, students are encouraged to discover and reach their full potential. The school district is doing its utmost to provide the opportunities to make that happen.

Taylor Independent School District serves around 3,000 students in the rural, agricultural, and manufacturing-based community located thirty miles northeast of Austin. The student-teacher ratio of fewer than 20-to-1 provides opportunities for individualized instruction and may be one of the reasons for the continuing rise in standardized-test scores.

Taylor's selection by the TEA to implement the Accelerated Model of Instruction has had an impact on the learning experiences offered. Students are immersed in technology. All district classrooms are networked and wired for Internet access; technological skills are integrated into the learning process beginning in elementary school. At the high school, the newly constructed science lab stations allow students to access science-related web sites as they work. Administrators have secured funding to perpetuate the provision of laptops for the district's ninth graders.

In addition to preparing students technologically, Taylor ISD has aligned itself with two different community resources. At Temple College a concurrent enrollment program enables high-school students to earn dual credit for both high-school courses and college-credit hours. A partnership with the Taylor Public Library makes possible the utilization of technology and research resources by residents. Laptop computers, provided by TISD, can be checked out overnight in a program administered by the library.

Taylor ISD is making the most of available resources. The result is passing marks for the students and the community.

RAMADA LIMITED

On one of Texas' scorching hot days in the middle of summer, the Ramada Limited might provide the perfect way for travelers to beat the heat. Located just north of Sam Bass Road along the west corridor of I-35, the Ramada Limited offers its guests the largest hotel pool in the area. Cathy Francis, hotel manager, says the 45,000-gallon pool is a real attraction for patrons of the hotel. The pool, however, is not the only appeal.

The Ramada Limited contains a little bit of history within its walls. The hotel holds the honor of being the site of the first hotel in the Round Rock area. It was not originally a Ramada, but rather the hotel bore the name of Round Rock's notorious bank robber from the 1800s. First called the Sam Bass Hotel, ownership has changed several times over the last twenty years, but the current proprietors, Ramada, seem to have found their market. Truck drivers in need of a place to rest find the Ramada extremely accommodating because of the generous parking provided for the big rigs. Another amenable feature of the hotel is its proximity to restaurants and shopping. Four restaurants are within easy walking distance, as is a shopping center offering a variety of retail establishments. In addition, those visitors who want to view Old Town and see firsthand the legendary round rock are just a few blocks away.

A healthy economy that has a low unemployment rate creates certain challenges for the hotel staff. Double- or even triple-duty is sometimes necessary in order to maintain a high standard of service and maintenance in the sixty-two-room facility. Ms. Francis is proud of the way her staff works as a team, pitching in wherever needed. This type of commitment enables the hotel to maintain its reputation for providing the cleanest rooms in town.

EMI

Reese Davis has watched Electronics and Metal Industries—the company he founded in 1975—struggle, find its niche in the electronics industry, survive tumultuous times, and ultimately enjoy success. Throughout, Davis has managed to maintain his integrity and instill loyalty in those around him. His sixty-five employees include not only workers who have remained devoted to the company that trained them but also trusted family members. Davis' cousin Bob Jones, an industrial engineer and now part-owner, joined the company in 1978, contributing his expertise and efforts to EMI's success.

Davis developed a solid technical background while working in Tennessee for Teledyne Systems, Inc., designing telemetry for the Saturn and Apollo missiles.

In 1975 Davis and wife Norma "Jeanne" returned to Texas, his native state, and purchased Omega Machine Products, a mom-and-pop machine shop located in the backyard of their home in Cedar Park. By 1984, Davis had relocated his business, initiated the company's electronics division, and bought out eleven companies. He merged all of them into EMI.

EMI manufactures electronics and metal systems on a contract basis, designing and building to fit each customer's particular needs. Providing services for many of the major companies in the Austin area has proven challenging. Among EMI's products are circuit boards for computers and zip-code readers; satellite cabling; touch-screen controllers for televisions; player piano electronics; and seismograph machines. A current project involves firewire, an innovation utilizing fiber optics that carries voice data at high speed.

Davis acknowledges that sound judgment and dedication have contributed to his success. Above all, however, he credits a positive trust in God and in His guidance. His priorities—church, family, work, and community—are reflected in the lifestyle he leads, including leadership roles in the Leander Church of Christ.

Since 1992 Davis' son Michael has been preparing for his future with the company. Perhaps that explains the twinkle in Davis' eyes as he speaks positively of the possibilities that may still await EMI.

❖

Above: Reese and Norma Davis.

Left: The company is located on FM 1431 between Cedar Park and Jonestown in an easily recognizable building that offers a beautiful hill country vista.

TXU

Electricity came to Williamson County on October 1, 1912, when Texas Power & Light Company acquired the electric facilities in Taylor from the Citizens Light & Power Company. The power plant consisted of a 350-horsepower Skinner Tandem-compound steam engine driving a 200-kilowatt General Electric AC generator and 150- and 125-horsepower Ball steam engines driving 110- and seventy-kilowatt generators, respectively. Twenty-two miles of distribution lines served 574 customers.

By the 1930s transmission lines linked the state's three largest electric utilities: Dallas Power & Light (DP&L), Texas Power & Light (TP&L) to the east, and Texas Electric Service Company (TESCO) to the west. In 1945, Texas Utilities was founded as a holding company for the common stock of the three utilities.

DP&L, TP&L, and TESCO merged in 1984 to become TU Electric. In 1995, TU went international with the purchase of an Australian electricity distributor. On April 15, 1996, TU and ENSERCH—former rivals—announced a merger. Completed in August 1997, the merger added natural gas to TU's services. Telecommunications was soon added to the portfolio with the acquisition of Lufkin-Conroe Communications in Southeast Texas. In 1998, another TU acquisition extended its electric/gas and energy services operations to the United Kingdom.

Today, the company has a new name—TXU. Headquartered in Dallas, the company's assets exceed $40 billion, placing it among the world's largest investor-owned energy services companies. Numerous Central Texas communities are served in one way or another by TXU, including the Williamson County towns of Georgetown, Granger, Hutto, Jarrell, Round Rock, Taylor, Thrall, and Weir. TXU—a multinational leader in electric and natural gas services, merchant trading, energy marketing, telecommunications, and other energy-related services—delivers energy to more than nine million customers.

Above: TP&L line crew, c. 1927.

Below: An early photo of Citizens Power and Light Company.

Round Rock Chamber of Commerce

The enormous growth that has characterized the Austin area in recent years has created a challenge for Round Rock community: how to avoid being swallowed up in the expansion process. As support system for its 800-plus member businesses as well as ambassador for the city, the Round Rock Chamber of Commerce, incorporated since May 1978, has assertively sought to create a tax base and a job base that would advance the city's plan to become a complete community. The healthy economy and enviable lifestyle enjoyed by the citizens of Round Rock tell the story of the success of the Round Rock Chamber of Commerce.

Looking ahead has been a key characteristic in establishing Round Rock's identity. The chamber undertook the task of implementing economic development strategies. Offering appropriately zoned sites and providing infrastructure needs proved to be invaluable. In addition, tax abatements and incentives attracted businesses to Round Rock. Phil Brewer, executive director, speaks proudly of the virtual "Who's Who" of desirable industries that have been brought into the community.

The variety of businesses has created a balanced economic base from which to address other issues. The Chamber has sponsored activities supportive to both businesses and citizens. In the late 1980's, the Chamber supported a campaign resulting in the voters' approval of a half-cent sales tax, to be used in reducing property taxes. In 1997, the Chamber again endorsed a successful half-cent sales tax referendum, this time to fund road improvements. The current "Shop Round Rock" program encourages consumers to do business in their city. Another program, Leadership Round Rock, provides an extensive series of seminars giving future leaders a broad overview of community services and a well-rounded knowledge of the community. The Chamber also began the tradition of Frontier Days, a fun-filled celebration of Round Rock's colorful history.

The first twenty-one years of the Chamber's presence in Round Rock have been productive. The growth predicted for the future promises more opportunities for the same.

Bo Brasfield, Broker/Associate
Donna Brasfield, G.R.I. Realtor

Bo Brasfield, broker/associate, and Donna Brasfield G. R. I. Realtor have been affiliated with the Coldwell Banker Richard Smith, Realtors for the past eight years, and in the Taylor office since 1996. This partnership has resulted in a substantial market share of the real estate transactions in Taylor. Bo and Donna believe they are in the business of providing service, and that belief extends as thoroughly to the smallest transactions as it does to the largest.

Three agents—Gil Elizalde, Jerry Ash, and Deborah Schernik—along with Bo and Donna, two assistants, a marketing director, and an office manager provide real estate services throughout the central Texas area. After closing 181-plus sales in 1999, the Brasfields expect that number to increase yearly. Business comes mostly from residential sales and farm and ranch transactions. The Brasfields are consistently acknowledged nationally for excellence. The Taylor office was named an international award-winning office in 1997, and both Bo and Donna produce sales ranking among the best in the nation. The Brasfields have been named to the Presidential Circle—representing the top three percent—as well as the President's Elite Club, a designation for the top one percent of all Coldwell Banker agents internationally.

Not content to rest on their laurels, the Brasfields constantly pursue ways to improve service. Making available both an in-house lender and an in-house title company provides convenience for homebuyers. The most recent addition to their services is the Coldwell Banker Concierge Program, designed to make home buying easier than ever by facilitating a variety of details that inevitably accompany moving into a new home.

Bo and Donna's office is involved in a variety of community-service activities, including the Adopt a Grandparent for Christmas program at the Taylor Care Center and the annual food drives. The office also participated in fund-raising efforts to support St. Jude's Children's Hospital. The Brasfields take time to actively participate in area Chamber of Commerce organizations as well as the Williamson County Association of Realtors.

Above: Donna and Bo Brasfield have been selling real estate in the Central Texas area for a total of seventeen years.

Left: Dedicated professionals make up the award-winning real estate team at Taylor's Coldwell Banker office. Pictured are (left to right): Nan Heeke, Bo Brasfield, Tiffany Bigon, Gil Elizalde, Jerry Ash, Candi Coughlon, Donna Brasfield, and Deborah Schernik.

Georgetown Chamber of Commerce

For over seventy-five years, the Georgetown Chamber of Commerce has existed to support businesses and professionals that in turn sustain the community. The group's broad-based mission includes: promoting member businesses and responsible economic development; providing leadership in business and community activities; communicating timely information on important matters; and creating a forum for understanding—and articulating—member perspectives on key issues. The challenges faced by a rapidly growing Georgetown are significant. The Chamber strives to be a partner with the community and its citizens in meeting these challenges while honoring Georgetown's unique heritage and its special quality of life.

❖

Above: The Williamson County Courthouse in downtown Georgetown and the Chisholm Trail marker in front of the historic structure.

Below: The Chamber's continued leadership in such vital areas as workforce development, education, business recruitment, and public policy, is critical to Georgetown's success and sustainability.

COURTESY C. SMITH PHOTOGRAPHY.

Like the community, the Chamber has enjoyed substantial growth in recent years. Current membership stands at approximately 700. The organization works both within its membership and within the community to accomplish its goals. Inside the Chamber, opportunities are provided for members to develop leadership skills through the Leadership Georgetown program. Monthly seminars offer timely and informative sessions for small businesses. In addition, networking opportunities are organized for members through various Chamber activities. The Chamber has impacted the community by focusing on issues that concern Georgetown residents. Chamber members are actively involved in studying new transportation proposals and in providing public awareness of the effects such proposals will have on quality of life. The Chamber supports economic development that conforms to the City's urban design standards and is consistent with community values. The Chamber's continued leadership in such vital areas as workforce development, education, business recruitment, and public policy development, is critical to Georgetown's success and sustainability.

The Chamber recognizes excellence through a series of annual awards, acknowledging contributions in all areas of Chamber activity. The Owen Sherrill Award for Economic Development—named for the man who established the Chamber in Georgetown and twice served as the group's president—is presented periodically. Such an acknowledgement, simultaneously honoring both past and present, seems appropriately representative of the role the Georgetown Chamber of Commerce plays in the community.

Wesleyan Homes, Inc.

In 1955, when the Central Texas Conference of the United Methodist Church committed to a ministry that would provide residential care for older adults, Don Scarbrough, then-editor of the *Williamson County Sun*, enthusiastically encouraged Georgetown citizens to provide a site for the proposed facility. A referendum election resulted in the City of Georgetown donating a city park to the United Methodist Church. On September 12, 1962, The Wesleyan opened its doors at the corner of Church Street and University Avenue. The four-story building provided two floors for independent retirement living, one floor for personal care needs and another floor for those requiring nursing care.

Increasing needs have necessitated several expansion projects. In 1978 an additional facility, dedicated to nursing care, was built at 2001 Scenic Drive on property donated by the Lola Wright Foundation. Another building project was completed in 1987, increasing the nursing home capacity to 180 beds. In 1999, an endeavor was undertaken to accommodate additional needs of the aging: a new structure adjacent to the existing Scenic Drive facility, providing special care for Alzheimer's patients.

Each new phase of The Wesleyan's growth increases its ability to serve older adults. The ministry's success lies in providing loving, dignified care on many levels—physical, emotional, and spiritual. Persons of all races and faiths, as well as people from all over the country, are welcomed into The Wesleyan's family.

The Wesleyan enjoys a mutually satisfying relationship with its neighbors in Williamson County. While residents of the various centers are recipients of volunteer efforts of numerous community and church groups, the community reaps benefits as well. Numerous independent residents offer tutoring services to elementary students. In addition, Wesleyan Nursing Center is affiliated with Georgetown High School, providing students with training and invaluable hands-on experience.

As it continues to successfully meet the challenges provided by an aging population, Wesleyan Homes, Inc. will undoubtedly remain a valuable asset to Williamson County.

Residents at The Wesleyan take advantage of the pleasant outdoor surroundings to enjoy an afternoon visit.

FTWOODS CONSTRUCTION

Todd Woods takes his business very personally. That quality has been instrumental in the success of his firm, FTWOODS Construction Services, Inc. With each new client, Woods and his staff concentrate first on building relationships, and then they build buildings. It is a formula that has worked well for the ten-plus years that FTWOODS has been in business in the Williamson County area.

Since October of 1989 FTWOODS Construction—with offices located at 1978 South Austin Avenue—has served clients in central Texas as design-builder, construction manager and general contractor. Achieving client satisfaction through teamwork and commitment is the chief objective of the company. The goal with each new project is to exceed the client's expectations and to deliver projects of the highest quality on time and within budget, while simultaneously maintaining a safe working environment. As testament to these lofty objectives, repeat customers compose eighty percent of the business. One client, the Georgetown Healthcare System, has utilized the services of FTWOODS for more than fifteen projects ranging from $100,000 to $11 million—including the recently completed hospital expansion.

Above: Aerial view of the Georgetown Hospital on Scenic Drive.

Below: Hal Investments office complex on IH-35 and Williams Drive.

In addition to managing healthcare ventures and participating in automotive, industrial, distribution and office/retail projects, the firm has had some interesting specialty projects. Among these are the Triple Crown Dog Academy in Hutto, the Don Hewlett Chevrolet-Oldsmobile-Buick Dealership, and the central U. S. distribution center for Texas Outdoor Power.

Even with the company's hectic pace, staff members take time to commit to a variety of community-service activities. Participation in philanthropic organizations, the PTA, chamber of commerce activities, fundraising for local youth organizations, and charitable donations are a few of the ways the FTWOODS' employees give back to their community.

Impressive examples of their work displayed prominently throughout the area as well as the accolades of satisfied clients suggest a bright future for the folks at FTWOODS Construction Services, Inc.

"At FTWOODS Construction, We Build Relationships...We Also Build Buildings."

Georgetown Independent School District

The corridor inside the Georgetown Independent School District administration building is known as the Wall of Fame. It is lined with letters with one thing in common: the communications from parents, TEA officials, former students, and community members were written to acknowledge something positive occurring within the school district. This wall provides an appropriate reflection on GISD. District Superintendent Dr. Jim Gunn, along with a dedicated board of trustees, sets high standards for the 600 teachers and 7,600 students in the district. The programs in place have produced higher-than-state-average scores on standardized testing. Yet the district continues to set objectives demanding successful learning experiences for every student in the district.

The first public school appeared around 1878. Boys and girls attended classes in separate facilities, boys at a sock factory located near the Presbyterian Church, where the girls' classes met. Several years later, public co-education had its beginning, providing classes up to eighth grade. Attendance was poor in part because some children continued to attend private schools which had been established earlier. In addition, while the first six months' schooling was provided free, the last three months required tuition; many students dropped out. In 1889, the black school was established, and the City Council voted to take over and administer the public schools, both black and white. By 1911, crowded conditions necessitated additional space; a two-room building, located where The Wesleyan now stands, was acquired. In 1916, the old Southwestern Building, used as a preparatory school by Southwestern University at the time, was purchased and used as Georgetown High School through 1922. In 1917, the Texas 35th Legislature established the Georgetown Independent School District, the name by which the school system is known today.

Growth, consolidation, and adherence to high standards have characterized GISD's place in Williamson County's history. The excellent reputation enjoyed by GISD and the successful life-long learners sent out into the world are evidence of the district's commitment to quality.

So are all those letters on the Wall of Fame.

❖

Above: Georgetown High School.

Below: The new Georgetown Independent School Districts' 1,200-seat Center for the Performing Arts.

Williamson County Historical Commission

Following an act by the Texas legislature in 1953 creating a State Historical Survey Committee to coordinate historic preservation with regional groups throughout the state, the Williamson County Historical Survey Committee functioned under the direction of County Judge Sam V. Stone until 1969, and Mrs. John Cornforth (1970-72). Since 1973, when the organization's name changed to the Williamson County Historical Commission, it has been chaired by Clara Stearns Scarbrough (1973-75), Dr. Van Tipton (1976), Myretta Matthews (1977-83), Laverne Faubion (1984-88), Leonard Wynn (1989), and Irene Varan (1990-).

Operating under the jurisdiction of the County Commissioners Court, by whom members are appointed, and the Texas Historical Commission, the Williamson County Historical Commission surveys, records, marks, preserves, restores, disseminates information about, and fosters appreciation for all phases of county history.

Past projects include compiling a list of Civil War veterans, and surveys of over 200 cemeteries. The commission has also placed 220 historical markers. Commission publications include three volumes of burial records and a map indicating the location of cemeteries and historical markers. The commission's newsletters and yearly scrapbooks provide valuable research tools. With the recent acquisition of a permanent headquarters building, current efforts are focused on establishing a county museum and archives.

Current members: Burney Downing, Laverne Faubion (vice chair), Mary Jean Livingood, Clara Scarbrough, and David Voelter (treasurer), have served over twenty years; Lester Fisher, Lerlene Ward, Irene Varan (chair), Ruth Olson and Elsie Waller, eighteen years or more; Margie Fullen, Dr. Lou Fullen, Hazel Hood, James Hood, Rod Johnson, Charlene Jordan, Ralph Dixon Love, Claire Maxwell, George Meyer, Sarah Myers, Larry Rydell, Barbara Stockley (secretary), Dr. Harold Weiss, Johanna Wimberly. Associates: Hugh Davenport, Anita Fox, Diane Pogue, and William Seward.

Above: Williamson County Historical Museum.

Right: Some of the 1999 members of the Williamson County Historical Commission.

Inner Space Caverns

Some businesses are created to answer a community's urgent need; others evolve from someone's lifelong dream. Inner Space Cavern, however, owes its beginning to an unexpected discovery made when Interstate 35 forged a path through central Texas. The discovery changed not only the course of the new highway but also the tourist industry in Williamson County. Inner Space Cavern has become a successful venture that currently attracts upwards of 125,000 visitors per year.

In the spring of 1963, pre-construction crews from the Texas Highway Department conducted core-drilling tests south of Georgetown to determine the ground's stability for the construction of a highway overpass. Initially workers found the expected solid limestone; below that level, however, the drill bit dropped significantly. Further testing revealed a large cave, formed because of its proximity to the Balcones Fault. A small group of businessmen recognized the cavern's potential and organized the Georgetown Corporation in 1963 for the purpose of development. Leasing the land from the Laubach family, the corporation proceeded with the development of the cavern. The discovery of new passageways led to many beautiful, new rooms. Eventually more than 14,000 feet of passageways were discovered, with approximately three-quarters of a mile now open to the public. Opening in 1966 for public tours, the cave was named to reflect the excitement generated by man's first lunar landing, which occurred in the same year as the cavern's discovery.

Visitors from the United States, Europe, Mexico, and South America are treated to a wide variety of speleothems, including stalactites, stalagmites, and helictites. Calcite crystals create other fabulous formations of many colors. In addition, bones of prehistoric animals, discovered within the cavern, have been the subject of many paleontological studies.

George Norsworthy now serves the corporation as president. He envisions a bright future for Inner Space Cavern as the corporation explores the possibility of developing new areas of the cavern while providing special programs to educate visitors and school children about one of nature's most intriguing and magical creations.

Above: A small "soda straw" formation.

Left: The Lake of the Moon.

Texas Pioneer Farm Mutual Insurance Association, Inc.

The log cabin built by S. M. Swenson in 1838 which stands in Zilker Park serves as a symbol of the proud Swedish roots of Texas Pioneer Farm Mutual Insurance Association, Inc.

A small cabin stands on the grounds of Zilker Park in Austin; an historical marker beside the structure describes its place in Texas history as one of the best-preserved log houses in the United States. Built in 1838 by S. M. Swenson, the cabin provided temporary housing for many Swedish immigrants whose passage to Texas had been financed by Swenson. Today, a likeness of the cabin serves as the official logo for an insurance company organized to meet the insurance needs of Swedish immigrants. Although Texas Pioneer Farm Mutual Insurance Association, Inc. now writes policies for property owners without respect to ethnicity, the connection to its Swedish roots is an integral part of its identity.

The insurance company that began as Goetha in 1911, established as its purpose the provision of fire insurance coverage for "the Scandinavian people in the towns and on the land in Williamson, Travis, and adjoining counties." The initial insurance in force was $150,000. According to a flyer distributed by Goetha, insurance protection was provided at the lowest possible cost "for the perils of fire, windstorm, hurricane, hail, explosions, riots, and civil commotions." The insurance offered no liability coverage. Licensed through the Texas Department of Insurance, Chapter 16, farm mutual insurance associations were created to provide insurance utilizing more lenient guidelines than those governing conventional insurance companies.

After merging with SVEA (in Travis County), Goetha became known in 1989 as Texas Pioneer Farm Mutual Insurance Association, Inc. Each policyholder is also an owner and is eligible to participate in both the election of the board of directors and the meetings held regularly to determine the direction of the association. The Round Rock office serves as the statewide headquarters for the association, supervising the underwriting of the $170 million insurance now in force.

Swenson might be surprised to see what has become of his efforts to assist his countrymen in their struggle to survive and become Americans.

Walburg State Bank

In August 2000 Walburg State Bank will have been in business for eighty-seven years. Although many aspects of the banking industry have changed, the financial institution's mission has remained the same: "We help people who really need help." Another constant in the bank's history has been the leadership of the Doering family. The consistency in both cases has offered stability for customers.

Henry Doering became the first president when the bank's doors opened in 1913. His grandson, Carl Doering, currently fills that role. Other presidents—who have served in between—include Julius Leschber, Dr. W. C. Wedemeyer, and Otto Doering. Presently on the board of directors are Carl Doering (chairman), Gene Lawhon, Steve Doering, Gene Jacob, and Jerry Pavlas. Lawhon is currently CEO; past CEOs have been Ted Walters, F. R. Leschber, and W. A. Kalmbach.

Present headquarters are in Georgetown on the corner of Austin Avenue and 11th Street. Branches are located on Williams Drive (Georgetown) and in Walburg. From three employees and $500,000 in assets in 1913, the bank has grown to over thirty employees and $70 million in assets. Recent growth has been at a rate of $5 million per year.

Walburg State Bank has survived everything from five bank robberies to difficult economic times and is the only bank in the United States never to close its doors during business days. Even during the depths of the Great Depression, when President Roosevelt ordered banks everywhere to take a two-day holiday, news traveled too slowly to reach the rural hamlet of Walburg until after the crisis was over. During another difficult economic time, other banks folded in the early 1990s; ironically, Walburg, in order to keep up with its growth, had to refuse deposits for one whole year.

A good neighbor in the community, Walburg State Bank has always supported charitable organizations. The bank appreciates the faith and trust placed in it by customers and has no plans to change the old-fashioned service for which it has become known.

TEACH

THE

CHILDREN

Walburg State Bank first conducted business from this site located in Walburg.

Chisholm Trail Special Utility District

❖

Above: Team 2000 Board of Directors. Front row (left to right): Bert Mansfield (president), Reg Pierson (vice-president), Paul Kugle, Jr. (director), and Phil Haag (attorney). Back row (left to right): Don Rauschuber (P.E.), Walter Doerfler, Jr. (secretary/treasurer), Howard Schaumburg (assistant secretary/ treasurer), C. E. Pastor (director), and Michael Smets (director).

Below: Team 2000 employees of Chisholm Trail Special Utility District. Front row (left to right): Danita Hawkins, Leanna Barr, and Maria Pasco; Middle row (left to right): Paul Medeiros, Patty Rodgers (general manager), Garland Nelms, Susan Weiss, and Billiejean Atkinson; Back row (left to right): Harry Randall, Ronnie Carter, Michael Rockett, Brian Cassidy, and David Owens.

The Chisholm Trail water supply system was developed by a handful of people who envisioned the need for a public water system to serve a beautiful but sparsely populated area covering 377 square miles west of IH-35 between the South San Gabriel River and the Lampasas River. The Chisholm Trail Water Supply Corporation, which began operation in 1984, became Chisholm Trail Special Utility District in 1992 with 1,300 customers. By the end of 1999 the District served 2,900 customers in the rural areas of Bell, Burnet, and Williamson Counties and the District had received 4,000 additional requests for water service. Although requests for service now come primarily from subdivisions and commercial customers, ranchers also rely on Chisholm Trail water for their daily consumption.

The original water system, funded by USDA-FmHA, transported water from the Edwards Aquifer to its customers. The current board of directors, engineers, lawyers and employees of the District, TEAM 2000, are seeking affordable water from sources such as Lake Georgetown and the Stillhouse Hollow Reservoir. They also are looking at aquifers located miles away in order to meet the ever-growing demand for water. Costs for upgrades and extensions for this new decade of project improvements are in excess of $28 million; the lion's share of which is being funded by developers.

The assumption that water sources would always be plentiful has given way to the reality of the necessity for conservation. The ever-increasing population inside the District's service area, along with stringent state and federal regulations, demands that the District not only continue to secure water for future use but also provide customers with conservation guidelines. Believing strongly that water conservation will become the foremost requirement in education for the future, TEAM 2000 has established a goal—"Conserving Water for All Our Children"—that includes working in the schools as well as in the community to educate the public about one of our most essential needs.

INDEX

Sponsors